SEVEN DECADES OF HUNTING, FISHING, AND TRAPPING

Also by Bob Erickson
Erickson's Outdoor Adventures

Series One: Hunting
Deer Stands and Stories

Erickson's OUTDOOR ADVENTURES

Seventy Years
of
Hunting, Fishing
& Trapping

Bob Erickson

Jack and Max
Enjoy sports and the outdoors
in your youth, and you will
have great memories for life

ERICKSON'S OUTDOOR ADVENTURES
St. Cloud, Minnesota

Bob Erickson

Duane Barnhart is an author-illustrator based in northern Minnesota. Duane's cartoon have appeared in *The Saturday Post, Mpls St. Paul Magazine, Lake Country Journal, Cabin Life*, and *Children's Magic Window* magazine. In the 1980s, Barnhart has drawn the nationally syndicated cartoon strip, *Can You Solve the Mystery?* He has designed print products and computer games as a freelancer for Warner Brothers and Disney. Duane has drawn editorial cartoons for the *Hudson* (Wisconsin), *Star Observer, White Bear Press*, and *Minnesota Daily* newspapers. He currently draws weekly cartoons for the *Aitkin* (Minnesota) *Independent Age* newspaper.

Copyright © 2011 Bob Erickson

ISBN: 978-1-936471-01-0

Pre-press by North Star Press of St. Cloud, Inc.

Printed in the United States of America

Published by:
Erickson's Outdoor Adventures
P.O. Box 7333
St. Cloud, Minnesota 56302
www.ericksonsoutdooradventures.com
e-mail: ericksonsoutdooradventures@gmail.com

Dedication

To my children and grandchildren

Acknowledgements

I want to thank my parents for their understanding and tolerance for my many unusual and not always pleasant adventures.

Taking few pictures in my youth, I was fortunate to meet and get the support of a great artist and cartoonist, Duane Barnhart. He was able to bring many of my experiences to life in a realistic and humorous way.

I want to thank Corinne and Seal Dwyer and North Star Press for their encouragement and support and help in preparing the book for press. Their knowledge of nature and the outdoors helped me formulate my experiences.

Contents

Part One: Trapping

Part Two: Bird Hunting

Part Three: Deer Hunting

Part Four: Fishing

Part One

Trapping

1

Looking Ahead

I GREW UP WITH A GREAT RESPECT for nature and our environment, but it started more out of necessity than appreciation. Growing up in the Central Minnesota town of Willmar, I lost my father in 1939, when I was six years old. I had a sister, Phyllis, age nine at that time, but no brothers.

In those years, there were few, if any, social programs to assist needy families, and my mother received only forty-three dollars a month from my father's life insurance policy. In order to make rent and feed us, she worked long hours. My sister and I were deprived of a happy family life. We were fortunate that our grandparents, Art and Ida Erickson, lived in Willmar and could give us some loving attention. Unfortunately, neither they nor any of our relatives hunted or fished to show me the excitement of these outdoor activities. I had to learn on my own.

My first experience in this world was when an older neighbor was trapping striped gophers and caught a weasel. He got an extra bounty for the weasel. I saw that little animal and that's all it took. I was hooked, and this ignited my interest in the outdoors.

In 1942, my mother married Herman Beck, and we moved to a farm ten miles north of Willmar. I was sad to leave my many friends in town for the lonely life of a farm, but it exposed me to the beauty of nature in a new way. Our farm was along the north shore of Mamre Lake, which, at that time, was more like a large shallow slough. I spend hours in enjoyment on that shallow body of water.

2

Eyeball to Eyeball

Herman's brother farmed on the east side of the lake, and his cattle used the lake as a watering hole and as a place to stand to cool off on hot summer days and keep the flies off their legs. As a result, the first thirty feet of the lake were cleaned of vegetation. Beyond that were reeds and rushes. In the summer, the lake grew a scum of green algae. Through the algae, I often saw the heads of painted turtles popping up. Dozens of them at a time on some days. I knew what they were, but I had never touched a turtle before. This provided an opportunity . . . and a challenge. Wading into the green water, I could get only to within ten feet of them before their beady-eyed heads would slowly sink into the water and disappear with a swirl of green wake. This got me more determined to catch one.

Returning to the shore, I stripped off all my clothes except my shorts and waded back into the water to try again. In the deeper water, even further into that green scum, and with only my nose above the surface, I could often get within two feet of the turtles. They were used to the cows, and not particularly alarmed by my head slowly inching closer to them. They couldn't see the rest of my body below the scum, so I was able to get

Eyeball to eyeball

eyeball to eyeball to them, so to speak, and they always had those beady eyes fixed on me when I did this. Then I figured out that, by getting two to three feet from them, I could reach out below the green algae and grab their bodies. My arms would be full of scratches from their sharp claws as they flailed about and struggled in my grasp, trying to escape, but I never had one bite me.

I would carefully examine my prisoners, their sharp eyes, long necks, and legs. I was surprised to find such beautiful colorations on their bottom shells, bright reds and yellows that had given these otherwise drab turtles their name. I was amazed how neatly their head, tail, and legs would

Painted Turtle

A painted turtle can win anyone's heart with its innocent eyes and bright colors. Though their shells are dark on top, on their undersides, they have bright colors—red, yellow, orange, and black—that often form striped designs. They don't rely on their hearing, but have great sense of smell and excellent vision. And they have a hypnotic gaze with their beady eyes.

Turtles are very old as far as species go, having been around for some fifteen million years according to the fossil record.

They are always found in or near water, preferring still ponds or slow-moving water to tumbling creeks or swift rivers. As they are reptiles and, therefore, cold-blooded, they are often seen sunning themselves on logs or rocks to warm up from the cold water. They are most active when their body temperature is 63 to 73 degrees. Sunbathing also helps rid them of parasites. In the spring, when they first come out of hibernation, they begin feeding at 59 to 64 degrees, but stop when their bodies reach 86 degrees. Painted turtles are mostly active during the day and sleep at night.

After they are sexually mature, female painted turtles leave their ponds in the spring to find a location to lay eggs. They prefer sandy soil and dig a hole with their hind feet, then lay five to fifteen eggs, then carefully cover up the hole. This process takes roughly four hours. That is the extent of the mother's involvement in her offspring, which incubate for seventy-two to eighty days. Temperature plays an important role in gender determination. With temperatures of 73 to 81 degrees, the eggs will produce males. Over 81 degrees and the majority of the baby turtles will be female.

In southern states females lay up to five clutches, but in the north, they usually lay one to two. If laid late in the fall, some eggs or hatchlings can survive the winter in their egg hole and emerge in the spring. In 2011, I found three hatchlings dead on roadways as they were crossing the road to reach water in late May. They are born with an instinct to find water, but are able to feed themselves from the moment they hatch.

Turtles recognize their home area. In an experiment, ninety-eight turtles were placed a mile or more from their home water. Forty-one returned.

Adults have few enemies—eagles and larger predators like raccoons, foxes and coyotes—but turtle eggs are preyed upon by rats, snakes, bullfrogs, herons, raccoons, skunks, and others. Young turtles have to contend with those predators plus eagles, crows, and hawks. But the biggest threat to young and adult is traffic on roads.

Painted turtles grow to five to ten inches across, with females slightly larger. Their diet consists of insects, worms, fish, vegetation, and carrion.

They hibernate by digging into the mud of ponds and rivers, but have been known to dig into wooded areas as well. Their temperature falls to 43 degrees during hibernation. Their life span is five to ten years, but have been known to live for thirty years.

fit back into their shells. After a good look, I would let them go, watch them swim away, then try for another turtle.

Coming out of the water, I was always green with scum, but the clearer water where the cattle had been helped and I splashed about in that until most of the green of gone. I spent several days turtling in this way during a hot summer week. Then came clothes washing day. My mother found my scummy shorts and immediately wanted answers as to what I had been up to. I told her all about the turtles, figuring she wouldn't have an issue with that activity. Mostly, she didn't, but she then explained to me what the cows also did in that lake besides drink the water and cool off. That ended my turtling right there.

3

Catch and Release

I WAS SORRY TO LOSE TURTLING as summer entertainment, but Herman was always kind and supportive of me. He showed me how to make a sling shot and encouraged me to dispatch some of the pesky barn sparrows that ate grain and pooped all over.

As I developed my skill with this simple weapon, the sparrows also learned to vacate when I came around. With fewer targets awaiting my deadly pebbles, I looked for other types of enjoyment. I soon found many small narrow paths in the long grass and weeds. I never saw any animal use them, so I figured they were being used at night. That became the challenge. How could I catch an animal that I would never see in the daytime. We had a post-hole digger that Herman used to fix fences when the cattle got out. I decided to set a trap for animals that had made the trails. I would dig a hole right in their path, and, in the dark, they would certainly fall in and not be able to get out. The post-hole digger made a hole eight inches wide, and I dug with it until my hole was eighteen inches deep. The sides of the hole were very smooth. I made sure to remove the dirt from the area and carefully covered the hole with a thin layer of grass stems to make the place look more normal, more natural.

The next morning I was eager to run out and see what I caught. As I neared the trap, I saw that the grass had collapsed. In the bottom of the hole was a mouse. It saw me and hopped wildly, trying to escape. Not wanting to get bitten by even so small a quarry, I went to the house to get a pair of leather gloves. I trapped the mouse under my palm, then closed my fingers around it and lifted it from the hole. I examined the small, frightened creature, then let it run off into the grass. I reset my trap. Over the next several days, I caught more mice, frogs, toads, fat spotted salamanders, and even a young rabbit. Each time, I examined the animal before releasing it into the long grass. Except for the young rabbit, most of the animals I caught in my pit trap had defenses, which I studied. The salamander was the most interesting. They would jerk their bodies from side to side while I held them in the leather gloves and excrete a liquid through their skin. I didn't test it, but I suspected it was either toxic or extremely unpleasant in the mouth of a predator.

It seemed I could always find entertainment on the farm, in the buildings, woods, grasses, and sloughs.

4

On Skunks

What's Happening?

ONE AFTERNOON IN LATE OCTOBER or early November 1942, I noticed more vehicles than usual racing up and down the gravel roads. They would stop near culverts, and people would get out and look in them. The traffic slowed by late afternoon, but at dusk, the vehicles returned, and they were driven recklessly. I didn't get it. The cars and trucks would stop at each culvert, and I'd see the beams of flashlights. I'd often hear the report of rifle shots then, and the vehicles would race off to the next culvert for more flashlight beams and shots. The next day I was told it had been the opening of skunk season. Skunk season? I asked what this was all about. Why

SKUNKS

Skunks were once valued for their fine, long, silky fur, but now they are mostly considered pests. About the size of a large cat, skunks seem larger because of their long tails and bushy fur. They are members of the weasel family.

Skunks seem cute and cuddly and show little fear of humans. They know their foul spray is a good defense. If threatened, they will usually run, but sometimes they become defensive. They face their threat, arch their back, raise their tail and stomp their feet. If this doesn't deter their attacker, as a last resort, they will release their anal glands in a spray that is often aimed at the eyes of their threat. They are offended by their own odor and vacate immediately afterward. In order to put themselves in spray mode, they stand on their front feet, turn quickly and hit the trigger. They have amazing accuracy and can launch their liquid assault up to fifteen feet, more if they have the wind in their favor. A hit in the eyes can cause temporary blindness, and the odor itself can cause nausea. Besides this rather effective weapon, skunks pose a risk because they are a common carrier of rabies. An animal not behaving in a normal manner should be avoided at all costs.

Skunks usually have four to seven young in an abandoned burrow, one they dug themselves, or find lodgings in rock piles, brush piles, culverts, or under buildings or trailer homes.

Like very large cats, skunks can obtain a weight of fourteen pounds. They are nocturnal, but sometimes will be out hunting during the day. They are omnivorous but especially like grubs, insects, small rodents, frogs, berries, and fallen fruit. They may hunt over an area of several miles, but they always seem to stay close to water.

In Minnesota, the typical striped skunk is the most common, but there is also a species of spotted skunk, or civet cat, which I have seen and trapped in my youth. I have not seen or heard of a civet cat in Minnesota in over forty years, but a few might still be around. These skunks are more common farther south. The civet cat is much smaller than the striped skunk, weighing in at only four pounds on average. They are excellent climbers, but, if threatened, they will do the typical skunk backstand before spraying.

Skunks hibernate in the coldest part of the winter when the weather is inhospitable and food is scarce, but they're often abroad early in the spring. Animals just out of hibernation are a bit dull and often are hit on roadways. This risk is not helped by the fact that skunks are planigrade, meaning they, like humans, walk flat on their feet, not up on their toes like dogs, cats, and many other mammals.

would anyone want to hunt such smelly animals? What were they good for? I began to learn.

The hunters were mostly older farm boys. They would drive along the roads, check the culverts for skunks in the afternoons, find which ones held them, then plan their evening. Several groups hunted the skunks, and they competed with each other in getting the most. It seems that skunks liked culverts. They would drag grass into the culverts, making a bed for the day, when they napped. After dark, they would emerge to go hunting. I heard that as many as seven skunks would use the same culvert for those day beds.

The skunk season was short, and it wasn't an easy prey to hunt. The season started at midnight, but the skunks would often leave their culverts at dark, so it was important to those farm boys to be ready. For some reason this was big sport for farm boys. Skunks could be a nuisance, and they carried rabies and got into chicken coops.

I don't believe game wardens were concerned that some of the boys shot skunks early in the evening. How would they know unless they too were waiting by the culverts? Some skunks were shot inside their culverts, and some would be chased or pulled out. What a smelly sport. Skunks killed inside the culverts were retrieved by using a long pipe with a length of barbed wire extending through it. A barbed wire ball would be made on one end, and a handle on the other. By pushing the wire ball into the culvert, it tangled in the skunk's fur. Turning the handle would ensnare it deeper into the fur. The the skunk could be slowly pulled out.

It was easy to tell which boys engaged in this sport. The odor clung to their clothes and vehicles, lingering about them for days, but the sport and the value of the furs made it worthwhile for a number of boys to hunt the striped animal. I believe they could get two or three dollars per hide, and most of the furs went to Japan.

In later years, the value of skunk fur dropped drastically. Today they have little value, which means there is little motivation for people to hunt them.

5

Mink

AFTER THE FIRST SNOWFALL, I NOTICED rabbit tracks on a rockpile near the lake. As we enjoyed rabbit on the menu from time to time, I set two rusty traps I found in the barn, hoping to catch a rabbit or two. The next morning, I set out to see if my traps had caught anything. Indeed, I had a nice rabbit in the first trap! The second, however, gave me a big surprise. I found a vicious brown animal held by the leg. I wasn't about to get close to its sharp teeth. Running back to the barn to tell Herman, I gave him a description of the beast I had trapped. He quickly surmised it was a mink, and went back with me, explaining

that mink had the most valuable pelts of all the animals in our area. He helped me dispatch the angry beast and showed me how to skin the animal and stretch the pelt. I got six dollars for that fur, and that was a lot for a farm boy. It was actually the day wage of a grown man. I had found some very rewarding results for my inquisitive interest in nature.

MINK

Mink are inquisitive members of the weasel family. They have a very good sense of smell, and they are wary of human scent, making them difficult to trap, but the rewards were considerable when caught. As they are almost always associated with water, their thick, waterproof coat is valued in the fur trade. But now, with the increase of ranch-raised mink, bred in a variety of colors, the value of wild-caught dark-brown mink has decreased.

The mink sport a dark-brown coat in the summer, but this changes almost to black in the winter when their pelts become prime. The animals often have a bit of white on their chins and throats. In size, the mink ranges from fourteen to twenty inches long and weigh one and one-half to three and one-half pounds.

As stated, mink like water, and dig a den in a river bank or on the edge of a pond, lake, or swamp. Sometimes they will use a hollow log that is located appropriately next to water, but are not above taking over the abandoned lodges of beaver or muskrat. They have three to four young in the spring of the year.

The diet for the mink includes mice, squirrels, muskrats, snakes, frogs, bird eggs, and fish. They are quick, aggressive hunters and are not afraid to take on prey their own size or larger. Much of their food they find in the water, and they have been known to dive up to sixteen feet for fish. Trappers often set traps at the water's edge

or even under water near the shore in mink terrirory as mink are always attracted to water, it being the home to most of their food sources. Mink are very territorial, and males will fight each other when terrirory lines are violated. Being related to skunks, mink can also spray intruders, but they don't have the range or potency of skunks, and they can't aim nearly as well. Personally, I think mink stink far worse than skunks.

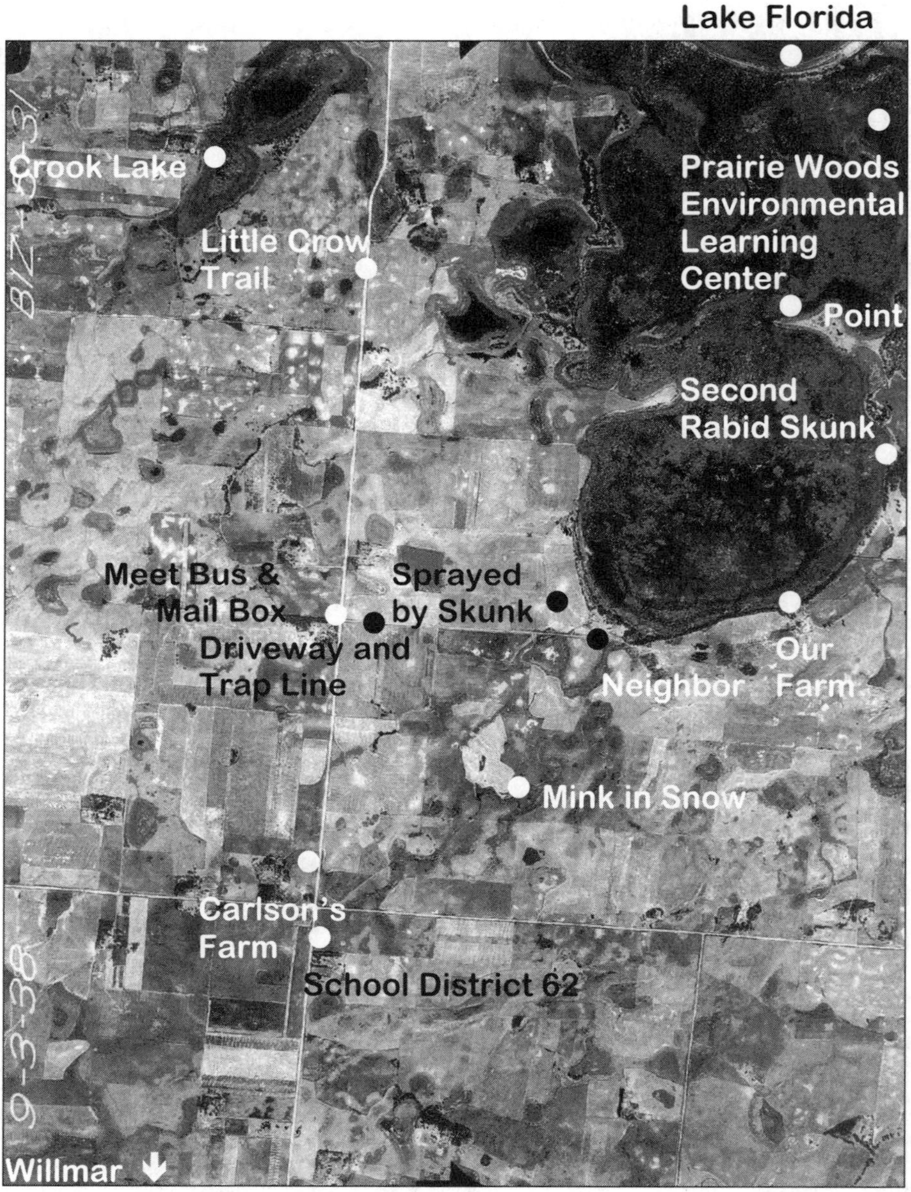

Lake Florida

Crook Lake

Prairie Woods
Environmental
Learning
Center

Point

Little Crow
Trail

Second
Rabid Skunk

Meet Bus &
Mail Box

Sprayed
by Skunk

Driveway and
Trap Line

Our
Farm

Neighbor

Mink in Snow

Carlson's
Farm

School District 62

Willmar ↓

6

Muskrats

Moving to Paradise

THE NEXT YEAR, HERMAN BOUGHT me six traps, and I trapped three muskrats and one skunk. I was bitten by the "trapping bug" and the income this could provide a country boy.

In the fall of 1943, Herman bought a small ninety-three-acre farm four miles to the east on the south side of Lake Flordia Sloughs. It was much larger than Mamre Lake and surrounded by woods, hills and small sloughs. It was a young trapper's paradise. With few people trapping at that time, I had permission to trap and hunt the neighbors' land as well, giving me a large area of opportunity. It also provided a natural "school trap line," I checked on my way to and home from school.

We had a narrow township road one and one-fourth miles long to the main main road, the Little Crow Trail, named after the Native American chief whose tribe once inhabited the area. The juncture of our long diveway and the main road was also the location of our mailbox. There was one other family on our township road, an older couple who had two older bachelor sons. We didn't realize until the first winter we were there that the township road was considered our private driveway

MUSKRATS

Muskrats are rodents as their name says, and they are probably the most common and prolific fur-bearing animals around, though the value of their fur has diminished significantly since my youth. The reason this rodent is value as a fur-bearer is because, like the mink and the beaver, it is a water animal, living, hunting and breeding near water. Their conical vegetative mounds rise above the water of ponds, and along the edges of marshes and swamps, but these are summer homes and tend to freeze up during the winter. They also use bank dens and usually have underwater entrances to avoid land predators.

Muskrats, being rodents, have multiple litters per year, sometimes up to five litters, though they average two to three in our northern state. Each litter is usually five or six kits, and individuals born in the early litters of the year can have their own young by fall. One muskrat was known to have produced forty-six kits in one year when the offspring of her spring litters were included. Clearly this is not a threatened species. Muskrat populations will vary, with fewer kits when the population is high or when food has become scarce.

Muskrats are clearly water rodents, and their tails are flattened vertically to use as a rudder when swimming. They hunt under water, looking for a variety of vegetation, including roots, stems, and buds. They are active during the day, mostly near dawn and dusk, but work right through the night if they are working to fatten their larder for winter. Their main enemies are mink, fox, coyotes, hawks, and owls. When threatened, they often dive down into whatever water they are near and can stay under the water for about twelve minutes.

Populations of muskrats can be estimated by counting the number of lodges in the area and multiplying by five. In the wild muskrats live to about the age of four.

and was not plowed, except that, in the spring, they would send a bull dozer out to scrape away the last of the snow. Otherwise we were on our own. With no bucket for our small "B" John Deere tractor, our main form of snow removal was a #14 grain shovel. Sometimes Herman would fix a wood plank to the front of the tractor to push the snow out of the way, but this method was of little use in the typical heavy Minnesota snow. After the first severe snow storm, we had to leave the road in some areas when they blew in and drifted too deeply. Then we would drive in the fields where the wind kept the snow depth down. After each snow and wind, we usually had to make a new trail where the wind hadn't created drifts. We had a 1939 Chevy car at the time. With chains affixed to the tires, that Chevy acted like our snow plow. Very little could stop it, and it could crash through drifts, blowing snow up over the hood and windshield.

In the winter with snow such an issue, we went to town about once a week, often after a full day or more of shoveling. To get to the school on the main road, I had to walk that long township road. I set my "school" trap line along the township road, and seeing what I had caught added interest, and sometimes excitement to my long walk. I caught mostly rabbits, which added to our menus, and skunks, which I sold for a modest income. My favorite trapping places were culverts near the neighbor's farm. It was a hot spot for rabbits and skunks. As I couldn't exactly deal with a skunk and then go to school, the neighbor helped me by shooting the skunks in the culverts for me.

Unexpected Excitement

ONE MORNING THE TRAP HAD BEEN PULLED into the culvert and out of my sight. I gently pulled on the anchor chain to see what I had caught. I quickly saw the black and white fur, but I wasn't concerned as most skunks ended up being caught by the front leg. This one was the exception and was caught by the back leg. It had its tail up, with its rear star-

ing me in the face, ready for action. Before I could drop the chain and step back, it let fly with its deadly weapon, catching me full in the face and in my eyes. I felt instant, intense pain and it blinded one eye. In just a moment, the fumes closed my other eye. I had seen our dog get sprayed in the face and go berserk. Now I fully understood the pain and suffering a skunk could inflict.

Unable to see, I stumbled back, falling against the shoulder of the road. I don't know how long I laid there in pain, nausous and wretching, before I got my vision back in one eye. I had to decide what to do. I really didn't want to go to school with the skunk stink on me, but if I went home, I had trouble, too. My mother didn't like my school trap line, but she had tolerated it up to this point. If I missed school because of it, she'd end it for sure. That actually made my choice easier.

The neighbor had seen some of what was going on and figured out what had happened. He came out and offered to shoot the skunk for me, so that part of my problem was taken care of. Not willing to lose my trap line over this, I plodded off down the road. The cold, crisp air began to help ease my pain and nausia, and it soon began to allow my vision to improve as well, well enough, at least that I could make my way along the road.

My Understanding Teacher

WHEN I ARRIVED, SCHOOL WAS ALREADY in session. I tried to sneak into the cloak room to get rid of my spattered coat, but the teacher caught me. She either had seen me sidle into the classroom or smelled me when I came in. She was a young teacher, about eighteen, and I can still see her face when she came around the corner, that look of abject shock that warmed into sympathy. I caught a slight smile on her face after that. I must have been quite the sight. My eyes were swollen, my face red, and I sure stank. She asked me to put my coat, cap, and gloves outside, then gave me a seat way in the back of the room as far away from the rest of the class as I could be.

Though my outer clothing took the brunt of the blast from the skunk, enough smell lingered on my person. All day, the other students would turn to look at me and laugh or dramatically hold their noses. To them it was funny. What had happened to me, however, most certainly had not been a lark.

That night I carried the skunk home, but I was careful to leave my outer clothes outside again, both to air them and downplay the extent of my contact with said animal. Mother knew I trapped skunks, of course, and was used to the odor, so I really didn't have to say anything more to her. However, at the school Christmas party, my parents heard about my incident from the neighbors, from other parents, and my fellow students. They were tactful, though, and let the whole thing slide.

Braving the Storm

On some days with less snow, I would cut across the fields to school, which allowed me to set traps for mink near a large slough. One night we had a heavy snow storm with blowing and drifting snow. The next morning, Mother thought I should stay home from school, at least until the wind let up, but I told her I had my traps to check, and after that, I might just as well continue on to school. Of course I worded my response so that school seemed the real motivation. That made Mother happy.

In those days, there were few snow plows, and they weren't used after every snow. With roads not plowed, kids stayed home from school a lot more than today. My two miles to school wasn't uncommon, but could be dangerous with high winds and blowing snow. Teachers would usually live at a nearly farm during the school year and walked to school as well. Sometimes after a storm, only a few kids would show up for school. I loved that. We played most of the day.

So, I "braved" the storm and headed off to check my trap line . . . oh, and to school, too, of course. Nearing where my traps were set, I came to tall cattails. Here the snow was two feet deep, making progress slow. The drifting snow had altered the landscape as well. Passing near one trap site, I noticed an unusual movement of one of the cattails. I stopped to watch the stalk wiggle, pause, then wiggle again. Digging down through the snow, I found a mink in my trap under the two feet of snow. It was caught by its toes and was struggling to get loose. It would have made it free, too, had I not checked the traps this nasty morning "on my way to school."

Lesson Learned

THE STORM DIDN'T LET UP THAT DAY. After school, Roger and James Carlson, who lived across from the school, asked if I wanted to stay at their house overnight rather than make my way home in the storm. I had never stayed overnight at anyone else's house before and quickly agreed. We had no telephone, so I wasn't able to call home. With our road blocked, I hoped Mother would understand and figure out what I had done.

My friends and I had a great time. The next evening, when I did get home to a rather worried mother, I told her it was the teacher's idea that I should stay over, and Mother seemed to accept that. A few weeks later, during another storm, I again decided to stay with Roger and James. Getting home the next evening, my mother wasn't as pleasant about this. She said, "If you can get to school, you can get home. I don't want to worry if you're lost." I came home, even in stormy weather, after that.

Odd Hole

MINK WERE THE MOST COVETED ANIMAL to a trapper. The highest prices were paid for those pelts. But mink also provided the greatest challenge to catch. Mink and fox both have a great sense of smell and paid particular attention to changes in their environments. Working against the mink, however, was their very inquisitiveness. They just had to poke their noses into everything.

23

My most unusual catch came from my lack of trapping experience and dumb luck. Walking along the edge of our slough and the wooded shoreline near our house, I was looking for fresh animal tracks as a light snow had just fallen the night before. I saw a few rabbit tracks, but then I saw strange hole in the snow-covered bank with no tracks around it, either entering or exiting. I got closer to examine it. The hole was about four inches in diameter in about a foot of snow. At the bottom of the shallow hole I saw a tunnel running both directions along the ground. Following this a bit, I saw an identical hole nearby, but again, no tracks. A little further down, I found some mink tracks where it had burrowed into the snow to begin the tunnel. This looked interesting, and I went home for a trap.

Breaking into the hole, I removed some snow along the ground and placed the trap at the same level as the bottom of the tunnel and off to the side of the hole. I then dusted some snow over the trap as concealment and tried to smooth the snow over my own tracks in the snow. I checked the trap over the next few days, but there was no action, and I saw no new mink tracks either. Then we got another foot of snow. Blowing again had altered the landscape, making me a bit unsure exactly where that trap had been set, but, as I had not had any action anyway, I decided to look for it when the snow melted in the spring. About a week later as we were hauling hay near that shore line, I decided to slide off the hay rack and look for new tracks. Near the trap location, I saw something dark extending above the snow, and it appeared to be moving a little. As I got closer, I saw that it was the tip of a mink's tail. A mink had found those same tunnels and stepped into my trap. It had tried to back out of the hole and the trap, but the snow had increased in depth and it had not been able to get to the surface. I discovered that it was a large male mink, the biggest I had caught. It netted me twenty-seven dollars. I later learned that male mink are very territorial but have a range of several square miles, which can take them several days to cover.

The tunnels in the snow I had discovered were used to hunt mice that stay active during the winter, living under the snow. The male mink in question probably returned to this location, discovered a strange scent and felt the need to renew its own markings.

My most productive mink sets were usually in water. That would hide my human scent and water was easily the favorite hunting grounds for mink. Small creeks were one of my favorite trapping areas in mid-winter, as even in the deep snow and severe cold, some sections would stay open. Open water was always a draw for roaming mink.

Last Chance

I HAD ONE SUCH CREEK THAT RAN THROUGH A MARSH, with heavy vegetation on both sides of the channel. I could always find some small areas of open water. This was located in the northeast corner of the slough about three-quarters of a mile from home. Because of the fewer hours of daylight in the winter and the need to get to school and back, I usually only trapped this area on the weekends. One year, with already over a foot of snow on the ground and a light snow forcast for that Friday afternoon, it was perfect conditions to set traps. Predators liked to be out in fresh snow looking for food. Either that or maybe they, like me, just enjoyed the new scenery. The creek was about 1,000 feet long, with about a dozen areas of open water. I set four traps, choosing areas where mink would have easy access to water. With the snow due to stop late that afternoon, it would make for great tracking the next morning. I was out early. As I neared the creek, I could see a few rabbit tracks, a weasel track, and then the tracks of a mink. I knew by the size of those tracks and the length of its stride that it was a large male. I followed it along the edge of the creek, checking all the areas of open water. I passed several such areas of open water before my first trap, and he had checked them all out. It was exciting to see where he had glided through the snow, heading down to the water and exiting with a leap up the bank, leaving a trail in the fresh snow.

I hoped to see him in my first set, but, according to his tracks, he walked to the edge of the water but seemed suspicious. He circled that small area of open water and then continued up the creek. I was disappointed I hadn't caught him but impressed with his caution. The mink continued along the creek, checking out all the open water but seldom entering it. As I came to my second set, I saw that he again had avoided the trap. Nearing my third set, I was already less optimistic about catching this wily mink, but I saw a bundle of brown fur in the trap. Rushing ahead, I was disappointed to discover that it was not the mink, but a muskrat. Muskrats were always attracted to open water. In the winter when the lodges tended to freeze shut, muskrats had to dig out of them. That made them easy prey for a number of predators. Such was their lot in life. But to discover the muskrat in the trap, I knew that the mink would have attacked the rodent had it been trapped before the mink wandered by, I knew the muskrat had been trapped after the mink passed. That meant that the mink had avoided that trap as well in its trip down the creek. I had little hope my last trap would prove successful if these first three had failed to snag the mink. As I neared the end of my short trap line, I could see no action near that final trap. Approaching the open water, I could see tracks as the mink had entered the water but no tracks where it had again exited. Getting to the bank above the trap, I saw a large male mink partially submerged in the water. That mink made for a great morning, with the muskrat as a bonus. One of the thrills of trapping is that you just never know what you're going to find and the day isn't a success or bust until the last trap is checked.

I found that setting traps in the few open, moving waters in the winter were the most productive. In severely cold weather, this can be a difficult process as well and is prone to problems. Traps can freeze over, requiring a trap relocation by breaking through ice. One small creek entering the slough always kept a small area of water open until the worst deep cold. Minnows would often come to those open spots, looking for oxygen, and mink came for the minnows. A mink had been making a regular evening visit there, too, attracted by the easy meal. This gave me a great opportunity. The mink would always fish along the edge of the ice, and with the flowing water and severe weather, the ice would expand or recede during the night. This meant frequent trap relocations for me, but I had success the third night.

Honesty

From the northeast corner of the slough, a point of land jutted out a quarter of a mile to the west, but another person had trapping rights to that land. Another small point of land on the west side of the slough across from this point was within my range, and I would often try it on weekends. When walking from my traps on the northeast corner of the slough to the west point, I would always walk on the ice to avoid the other person's traps. I approached the west point one morning to see a man step out of the cattails and accuse me of checking his traps. I told him I hadn't, but with no snow it was impossible to show him that my tracks hadn't gone anywhere near his traps on the east point. I walked with him to his traps as he continued to insist that I had checked them.

Getting near his traps, we both could see that something had been caught in each of his two traps, which were about six feet apart. One held a mink and the other an owl. The traps had been set in collapsed muskrat tunnels, always good places for looking for food for both minks and owls. Apparently the mink and owl had been looking for prey and got caught while doing so. They may have intended to make a meal of the other. At least this proved I hadn't checked the man's traps.

He Has to Live with It

Another year I was trapping near the northeast corner of the slough under some tree roots where the soil had eroded. It was like a small cave, with roots hanging over the entrance. These were always great attractions to rodents, which, in turn, attracted the predators. I set a trap in the cave, but instead of staking it down, I made a drag set. I attached a foot-long stick to the chain loop so that the animal could drag the trap away from the set and get hung up in the surrounding brush where it would be easier for me to get at them. By leaving the set area, the caught animal would not tear up the area, possibly ruining it for a future set.

Having no luck on the weekend, I left the trap during the week, but because of the distance from the house, I couldn't ckeck it in the morning before school. I had to check it quickly after school before the light failed.

We had gotten a light snowfall the previous night, and as I approached the cave, I could smell mink—a very good sign. Approching the tree, the ground and snow had been torn up by something caught in the trap. There was the heavy smell of mink, but also dog tracks and no sign of either the trap or the mink. Checking the fresh snow, the only tracks were the mink coming in and the dog coming, then leaving. I followed the dog's tracks and could see marks made from my drag stick as well, as if the dog had the mink in his mouth and was dragging the stick behind him. It was well past dusk, but with the fresh, white snow, I could easily follow the tracks. The dog headed northeast into the woods, into an area I had never gone. The dog took what looked like a straight line to somewhere, like it knew exactly where it was going. I stayed on the trail. After about half a mile, I saw a dim light and came to a mobile home. Again I caught the scent of mink and knocked on the door. A man answered the door, and I explained my problem. I asked if his dog had brought home a mink in a trap. He said no, but that his dog had come home with a trap on his foot. He then went to a shed and offered me the trap. There was a heavy smell of mink in the shed. I figured there really had been a mink in the trap.

I had never seen this person before or his house, but I took the man at his word and went home. In the light of the kitchen, I could see that the trap had mink hairs in the jaws. The man had lied to me, but as I was only fourteen and had to live with his adult choice. I didn't have to be happy about it, though.

7

Weasels

Tight Fit

MY UNCLE KELLY LIVED ON A FARM with an old-style ice box (a refrigerator) on his porch. As it required ice, it was seldom used in the summer, but as the porch was not heated, it was often used in the winter as an ice box. For two mornings in a row, the uncle found something had gotten into the ice box, gnawing on some of the frozen meat. It was an animal larger than a mouse, he figured, and set a rat trap inside the freezer. He caught a small weasel. Resetting the trap, he caught another one the second night. The ice

WEASELS

Weasels, related to mink and skunks, are much smaller, usually weighing one to one and one-half pounds. They are inquisitive, quick, and don't much worry about people being around. And, yes, they too can produce a foul odor. Weasils sport a brown coat in the summer with a bit of white at the throat and a black tip to their tails. In the winter they turn white but keep that black-tipped tail.

Weasels live in burrows abandoned by other animals, and have litters of four to eight. Their diet is carnivorous, like the mink, feasting mostly on mice. Unlike the mink, they are not as water oriented, though they are often found in the rough land of swamps and marshes. Because of their rodent diet, they are a considerable benefit to farmers even though they can get into trouble in hen houses. They are usually nocturnal, but will often hunt several hours during the morning and evening when the sun is up. They have been known to chase and catch squirrels in trees—no mean feat—and, when they gain access to chicken coops, can seem to go on killing sprees, dispatching chicken after chicken because the killing is so easy. People think they drink the blood of chickens when they do this, but chances are they just get a little nuts with all those hens squawking and flapping about them. Still as fast-moving little predators, they consume twenty-five to forty percent of their body weight in meat each day.

The shape of the weasel is long, lean and slender. They can get in surprisingly small holes and are formatable predators for their modest size. If their heads fit, they can get into almost any building, but their main purpose isn't to slaughter chickens but to reach the mice that also use the small holes. For every chicken a weasels has killed, hundreds of mice have been taken, making them more friend than foe.

box had a small pipe to drain off melt water, and that pipe had provided entrance to the small weasels. As there weren't many weasels in the area, and they were of low fur value, I seldom trapped them. Still I found an efficient way to get them. I would take a common rat trap—with the wood base—and nail it to the top of a wood shingle or piece of board, with the trigger end toward the bottom. I would bait the trap with a dead mouse (taken in a mouse trap usually), a dead bird or piece of raw

Bob Erickson (Willmar, 1946) with his wall of skins. These include one weasel, three mink, 20 muskrats, and nine skunks.

meat or suet. I would lean the shingle or board against a tree or, in deep snow, push the end of the shingle into the snow. Simple, but this was very effective.

Skunks were always easy to catch, and had a fair price for their pelts, but, because of the smell, not too many people trapped them. After my experience, I knew why, thought even that nasty event didn't keep me from hunting them. Skunks seemed to ignor human scent, which make trap preparation a lot easier, and, since they had predictable habits, they were pretty easy to locate and trap. One year I trapped thirteen of them. Herman told me how to skin a skunk, but he didn't help. It wasn't a pleasant job, but my eyes stayed on that two to three dollars I'd get for the skin, making the nasty job easier and making the lingering odor tolerable. Herman did help me build some fur stretchers, and I would stretch the furs and leave them in the corn crib to dry.

Not Pleasant!

Up into the 1950s, Sears and Robucks bought raw fur pelts. I would sell a few furs locally, but as I trapped larger numbers of animals, it was worthwhile to ship the furs to Sears. Looking for any additional income I could, I sent them a surprise when I was thirteen. We had two farm cats die during trapping season, and I saw the possibility for more income. I skinned the cats and sent those skins along with my regular fur shipment to Sears. Sears had a standard form where they listed all the animals in the state. For each species I sent, they checked off the number I was including, the size and the price. On the bottom of the form was written: "House Cats – Calico – 10¢, black, 20¢."

That winter we also had a calf stillborn out in the pasture. I dragged it home and hung it up in the barn to thaw out. A stillborn calf is not pleasant to look at, and also not so pleasant to skin. I had never had a messier job, but the hide sold for $1.50, well worth the effort.

Could Have Been Fate

Coming out of the house for chores one morning in early September, I encountered a skunk chewing on the metal hopper of a corn elevator. That seemed odd to me. Cautiously approaching the animal, I

33

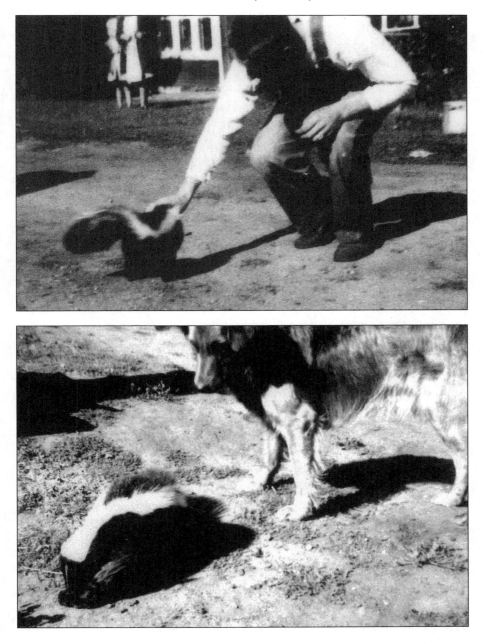

saw that one of its eyes was completely closed, covered in puss. Only a slit of eye showed through the other one. And, it was slobbering at the mouth. Further, it totally ignored me, so I got a stick and rubbed its back to get some reaction. I got none. Thinking the animal might be hungry, I shot a black bird to feed it. The skunk attacked the bird readily enough, tore it apart, but it didn't eat it. As it wasn't offering to spray me, I grabbed it by the tail and lifted it off the ground. It just twisted its body slowly. It seemed sluggish, though it did try to grab my leg. Placing it back on the ground, I grabbed it across the back. It turned toward my hand, trying to bite me, but didn't get very far with that either.

My mother and two half sisters were interested, but they kept their distance. The dog, Shep, also seemed interested in this odd skunk, but instinctively he kept his distance.

With chores waiting, I placed the skunk in our dog house, shutting him in with a piece of chicken wire fence so he couldn't escape. The next morning, the skunk was dead. I threw it down by the slough.

Second Chance

TWO WEEKS LATER WAS THE OPENING of duck season, and I was walking along the east side of the slough looking for ducks when I saw a skunk walking on a cow trail cut into a side hill in the pasture. I watched it stumble, slide back down the hill, scramble back to the trail and walk a short ways, then stumble again. I investigated. It also had puffy, cloudy eyes and a slobbery mouth like the skunk two weeks earlier, but this one was in slightly better condition.

I always enjoyed playing jokes, and this skunk would provide a good one. I would lose some good duck-hunting time, but it was a once-in-a-lifetime opportunity. It was nearly half a mile to home, but I picked up that skunk by the tail, holding it at arm's length so that its twisting and turning wouldn't give it access to my legs. It tried hard to claw at me. Holding a twelve- to fourteen-pound animal at arm's length isn't something one can do for very long, but I managed to get home with the skunk and without bites or scratches.

Mother wasn't pleased to see me come home with a live skunk, but after I explained my plan, it took her only a few seconds to go along.

About eight duck hunters' cars were parked in our yard, with Kent's, one of my two favorite hunters, on our lawn in front of the porch. I found a small cardboard box, put the skunk inside and taped the flaps shut. On top of the box, I wrote "To Kent from Bob," and put the box in the driver's seat of Kent's car.

Mother helped on my vigil, waiting for Kent to return from hunting. I saw him first and called Mother, and we both watched from the front porch, careful to stand where Kent couldn't see us.

Coming up to his car, we watched as he opened the door and saw the box. He looked a little confused. He set his gun against the car and reached for the box, giving it a good shake. He read the note and ripped off the tape. Mother and I watched as he opened the flaps. As they came up, so did the skunk's tail.

Kent jumped back, yelling something we couldn't quite understand, which was probably lucky. Mother stayed on the porch, but I ran out to Ken't car, laughing. He didn't see the humor in the situation. He glared at me and yelled, "Get that damn thing out of my car!"

The excitement brought some other hunters up from the slough, and there was only silence as I took the box out of the car. I reached into the box and grabbed the skunk by the tail and lifted it out. For fun, I started in the direction of the other hunters.

They stepped back but quickly began laughing as they saw the serious look on Kent's face and my lack of concern. I explained that I had found a skunk just like this one two weeks earlier and it had died the next day. They offered to shoot it, assuming it was also dying.

Bad News

Two weeks later, a nearby neighbor had a cow die. He called the vet and was told that the cow had died of rabies. We didn't connect the two ill skunks to the dead cow until another couple of weeks passed and we had a steer die. We also called out the vet, and he told us it was rabies.

I told the vet about the behavior and condition of the two skunk, and he felt confident that they also had been inflicted with rabies and was concerned about me. He said it was too long after possible infection for any preventative medicine, but since I hadn't been bitten or scratched, he told me I had been very fortunate. He cautioned me against playing with more sick skunks.

In just handling the skunks, he said I was lucky I got none of the skunks' saliva into some scratch or wound. Rabies, he warned, was nothing to take lightly as it was usually fatal.

This year, 2011, I heard of the first case in the United States, where a person recovered from rabies with no medication.

I know I was fortunate not to have gotten sick. I was also lucky it was a month before trapping season when I found those skunks. I would likely have skinned and sold their pelts, probably infecting myself in the process.

About Rabies

A few years ago, I met a veterinarian from a nearby town, and he passed along information about rabies. It's a disease, a virus, that is almost always fatal. It affects the brain and paralyzes the muscles, causing them to contract. This makes it difficult to swallow and breathe. Any movement aggravates the effects. In animals, rabies will cause the lower jaw to stiffen and hang down, causing drooling. Animals also become nervous and excitable. Oneway to check for rabies is to quietly walk up behind the animal and clap your hands or make some loud noise. If affected, the animal will react nervously and charge any movement. I believe my skunks were too far gone to have much reaction.

Rabies-affected cows show less aggression. They can't swallow and get lethargic. Dogs get a locked vision. If they follow someone, their head will move from side to side to follow each step.

The main carriers of rabies are skunks, foxes, raccoons, and bats. Gnawing animals, such as squirrels, beavers, rats, and mice (rodents) are much less prone to rabies. In most animals, death comes in thirty to sixty days after first showing signs of the virus, but bats can survive several years as carriers of the virus before infecting a victim or dying of the disease.

The virus must enter the body through a bite wound, a cut, or scratch. The further the infection site is from the brain, the longer the animal (or person) takes to show symptoms. It may take a month or two for any ill effects to show up.

The test for rabies involves examining of the brain of the affected animal. This requires that the animal be euthanized. If the animal died but is not too deteriorated, exams results can are still good.

In the past decade, fewer than six human cases of rabies are reported each year. But the disease remains endemic in wild populations of animals with breakouts here and there annually. Recently, a bobcat charged people riding a golf cart. The golfers killed the bobcat with their golf clubs. It was tested and found to have rabies.

When someone has been exposed to rabies, vaccine shots must begin within a week of the incident. When I had my experience, the vaccine for rabies was given with a long needle inserted in the folds of skin of the stomach wall. I was shown the needle used for the shot, and it was several inches long. They said it went "into" the stomach. It had me worried.

As the shots caused severe swelling, itching, and irritation, they were not given in the arm. To spread the vaccine over a larger area of the stomach, doctors would insert the needle and then disperse the vaccine as the needle was withdrawn. It would take a series of these painful shots to kill the virus. The only reason I escaped this procedure was that my exposure had been weeks past. The vaccine would have had no effect if I had contracted rabies.

The first rabies vaccine was developed in France in the 1800s. Raw potatoes were used as a host to develop the vaccine. In about 1948, American Cyanamid developed a new vaccine that was easier to administer and had less irritation. The first large-scale tests were made in Saudia Arabia because many people there contracted rabies from their camels. Camels can normally be irritable and tend to snap and bite. Affected by rabies, this behavior gets much worse. The study involved a group of people who had been bitten by infected camels. They were divided into two groups to test the vaccine. One group was given the vaccine, while the other received a placebo. Those given the vaccine all lived. The others all died.

Nowadays a preventative vaccine can be given to those who are around animals and subject to infection. It is a series of shots, but the protection will last several years.

8

More Muskrats

New Adventures

I TRAPPED A FEW MUSKRATS in Mamre Lake but it lacked cattail and reed growth and supported few rats. The move to Florida Sloughs gave me better trapping opportunities as this was a much larger body of water, with many more small sloughs in the surrounding hills. We lived on an area called a "glacierial ridge," hilly terrain caused by the glaciers when they melted and dumped piles of material with numerous depressions that

became lakes and sloughs. There were small areas of vegetation in most of the sloughs where muskrats built their summer lodges, with bank rats along lakes and streams.

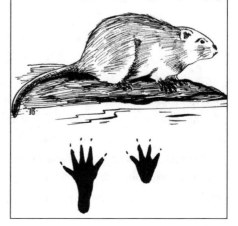

Muskrat were my favorite animal to trap as they were abundant and easy to trap. As they moved around most hours of the day, I checked my traps twice daily. The season for muskrat usually opened after ice had formed and much of the other trapping had slowed down. Muskrats would build their lodges in areas of vegetation, and, usually, the more vegetation, the larger the lodges. Inside they had living quarters on a platform also constructed of vegetation set above the water level with a tunnel that exited under the water. The walls of the lodge could vary from about six inches to well over a foot. To set a trap, I had to chop through the wall with an ax or chisle. I got so I could guess by the shape of the lodge where the thinnest wall would be, and I was usually correct. I would set the trap near the water entrance, trying to keep it level with their living platform. To anchor the trap, I would attach a six-inch long lath to the ring on the chain and lay it across the hole chopped into their den. The lath helped to plug up the hole I had created and make it look more natural as I sealed the hole with the chopped out vegetation, or some pulled from the lodge.

Much muskrat trapping was done in below-zero weather, and it was important to seal up the entrance hole so the muskrat's water entrance would not freeze up, forcing the rats out of their lodge. When ice kept them out, they seldom survived. It was difficult to find food and shelter deep in the winter, and wandering in the open made them easy prey for hawks, owls, foxes, and cars.

On the farm we had a flowing spring, thanks to the hills. We piped that water into a wooden trough for our cattle and pigs. One winter a muskrat found refuge in the trough. He was there two days, but then we believe it was killed while searching for food.

Great Experience

MANY YEARS LATER, WHEN I LIVED on the outskirts of St. Cloud, Minnesota, we had a beautiful small slough across the road. One afternoon during a snowfall, our son Lowell was walking home from visiting his friend Pat. He was crossing the slough when he saw fresh muskrat tracks in the snow. Trailing it through some cattails, another animal track soon appears coming in from another direction and also followed the muskrat. After a short distance, Lowell saw evidence of a struggle, some blood, and then a trail in the snow where the rat was dragged towards the woods. Following that trail, Lowell came to the base of a tree, where he found the rat. There was some blood on the side of the tree trunk where a mink had tried to drag the rat into a squirrel hole, but it wouldn't fit.

Lowell brought the muskrat home. The next morning, he went back to the tree to see a mass of fresh track all around the tree and into the woods where the mink had searched for his muskrat.

On Easter morning one year, Lowell went into that woods to observe nature and came back with a fresh-killed rabbit that was missing its head. I suspected an owl. When I removed the skin, we could both see punctures and long scrapes in the flesh. Lowell said he had found the rabbit at the base of a tree with blood on the bark that looked like it had dripped from an upper branch. I asked him to return to the location and look for the head. He returned with a skull that was missing the eyes and all the meat. Owls swallow their prey whole or, in the case of a rabbit, in chunks. Then they regurgitate the bones after the flesh has been digested. The owl had severed the rabbit's head from the body, and then picked the skull clean. That was apparently a choice part of the rabbit.

Muskrats are often seen out in the open in the spring. This can be caused when water rises with the spring melt, flooding their lodges and bank dens. Also, individuals, tied to water much of the time, must find mates and a location to build a new home to raise their family. That often puts them well away from the water, often on roadways.

When I was a boy, there were fewer regulations about how to obtain muskrats. Some would spear them. When the ice was clear and thick enough to walk on, people would tip-toe out to a lodge, stomp on it, then watch where the rats exited under the ice. Their shapes could be seen through the clear ice. After several hours, when the rats were supposed to have calmed down and returned to their lodge, a team of hunters would silently walk to the lodge. As one got ready over the exit tunnel with a single-prong spear, the other would stomp again on the lodge. The frightened rats would dive out of their lodge, only to be speared. This was sometimes done as entertainment as well as for the fur, but the pelts were less valuable with spear holes.

On warmer, sunny winter days, rats would often sit up on the ice near an open hole, eating. Some people would shoot them with .22 rifles, but if the rats dove or fell into the water, even wounded, they were often lost. Trapping was a surer method and produced an unpunctured pelt.

I usually had success the first day of trapping, sometimes gathering as many as seven rats out of one lodge, though the usual was two to four.

Occasionally I encountered a "wise" rat who played with the trap and snapped it without being caught. That would create a challenge for me, trying to hide my trap better or even hanging the trap in the water by the exit. I won some contests, but lost some, too.

Muskrats often had "feeder" piles scattered on the ice around the lodge. These would usually be about eighteen inches to two feet across with just enough room to sit and eat before diving back into the water to return to their lodge. I would sometimes trap the feeders, but I had to be careful. Most had very thin walls and tended to freeze up very quickly with the first severe weather.

Having to check the traps twice a day, and having some trap lines over a mile long, I would often start at five in the morning so I could get back in time to get to school. I would leave some still longer trap lines for the weekends.

With a small amount of snow on the ice, I would sometimes ride my bike to check the traps.

Muskrats can be vicious, but I usually used only my bare hands to set and check the traps for better control of the trap in the dark dens. Still, I only had one severe bite, and one embarrassing one.

One rat had a broken tooth, and, in biting my thumb, tore out a small piece of flesh, leaving it hanging only by a piece of skin. I was at the northeast corner of the slough, but I was lucky to have my bike with me that day to make a quick ride home. Popping the flesh back in place and holding it in with my finger, I rode home, leaving a trail of blood in the snow. Mother wrapped it tightly in a Band-Aid, and I returned to complete my trap line. The wound caused a problem, as it wouldn't attach, and I had to keep changing Band-Aids. When I took the bandage off, the chunk of flesh popped back out. It took over two weeks before it stayed attached and healed.

The embarrassing bite came later. I had caught a rat, and, thinking it was dead, threw it behind me as I reset the trap. It wasn't dead and wanted to get back into its lodge. I was in the way. It rushed up and bit me in the butt, but, through all my clothes, it didn't break the skin.

Because of school, I was limited in the area I could trap. I usally caught twenty rats a year. After graduation from high school in 1951, I went to work on the ore boats on Lake Superior for the summer to make money for college. When the ore boats ceased running for the winter in late November, I went home for the start of a fifteen-day muskrat season, beginning December first.

I was fortunate that three of Herman's brothers had adjacent farms along Crook Lake, which was mainly a large slough and only three miles away.

I found a fair number of rats along their shore, but a portion of the lake was open to public trapping. I bought some traps to bring my total to thirty, and wanted to get a few traps on the public area of Crook Lake before others thought of it. As most of Florida Slough was also open to public trapping, I needed some early help on Crook Lake. Herman offered to set some traps on the open area of the lake, and I would come back later and set some on his brothers' shore.

Getting to Crook Lake in the early afternoon, I set traps along the brothers' properties, and then went looking for the seven traps Herman had set for me on the public land. He had explained where they were. I opened one lodge and found a trap, but I could see it wasn't my trap by the stick and the ring. I closed up the lodge and went to find my other traps.

45

I Didn't Do It

As I was walking back, another trapper came over and asked if I had checked one of his traps. I told him I had but saw it wasn't my trap and left it. I said I thought I had seen a rat in the trap. I explained that Herman, who he knew, had set the traps for me and I hadn't known exactly where all of them were. I walked with him back to the lodge. We opened it, and, indeed, he had a rat in his trap. That appeased him.

I was fortunate that, as I trapped out some lodges, there were others around to set my traps in. If there was no action for a day and a half, I moved my traps to other lodges. Being able to adjust some traps, I was averaging about twenty rats per day. Still, I put in long days that would start about six in the morning and end about eleven that night. After I got home from one trap line, I had to skin all the rats I trapped and stretch the hides, then go out to check another one. Anything I caught would have to be skinned and stretched later that night. I made about forty fur stretchers out of wood shingles and would place the hides on the stretchers and set them on our front porch where they would freeze and dry. I could remove them from the stretchers in about thirty-six hours so that I could reuse the stretches on newly trapped rats.

I had a surprise one morning as I approached a lodge. A mink was peering out at me from a small hole it had made in the lodge. It had burrowed into the lodge after a rat and had gotten caught in my trap.

By the fourteenth day of the season, the weather had gotten colder, with temperatures falling to fifteen below. Some of the lodges began to freeze up. I had a hard time finding material to plug up the holes I chopped in the lodge to set the traps. I couldn't keep them from freezing up, and I didn't want that. I pulled my traps.

My uncle's land included a small slough that usually dried up in the summer, but this year it had water. I found two muskrat lodges and a feeder pile. Setting traps in each pile, I caught four rats each of the first two days, three the third day, and two more the next. What was unusual was that, even in the bitter cold of the last few days, the holes in the

46

lodges were packed with small minnows. With the heavy snow and ice, they were coming up for oxygen. I wondered how they got there in any numbers, as this slough was on higher ground, had no creek, and was often dry in the late summer and fall. I assumed that waterfowl had somehow brought in some fresh eggs on or in their bodies, but I really don't know how the minnows got there.

At the end of fourteen days, I had 306 muskrat skins and one mink. I don't recall the price of the mink, but I averaged ninety-three cents each for the rats, sending them to Sears and Robucks.

9

Raccoons

Then Uncommon

Where we now have many raccoons, fox, and coyote living on the farm, in the forties and early fifties, there were very few. We had no coyotes, and despite my roaming the hills, I never saw a fox, but I knew there were a few around. I would have liked to, but never trapped a raccoon, and only saw them twice while on the farm. Once Shep discovered one in a brush pile, and one came out of hibernation during a warm spell in the winter.

I had an experiece with raccoon many years later, when visiting my parents on the farm near Paynesville. they had

a chicken coop behind the barn and were having trouble with some animals coming at night. A few chickens had been killed, and the whole coop got riled up night after night. We parked the car on a small hill overlooking the coop with the headlights focused along the ground at the coop. My cousin and I each had a shotgun.

We checked the coop every few minutes after dusk by turning on the headlights, but there was no activity until near midnight, when chickens started to fly around and squawk. Turning on the headlights, we saw two raccoons leaving through the trees. We shot at both.

Flashlights in hand, we found one large female raccoon and looked for the other one. Shining the light up into the trees, we spotted some eye glare. We shot that animal, but it wasn't a raccoon. It was a civet cat. It had been about twenty feet up in the tree. I'd had no idea civet cats actually climbed trees.

That ended the raiding of the chicken coop, but I had some bad news later. The next week, Herman found a baby civet cat dead in the cow yard, probably the young of the one I shot.

RACCOONS

Larger than the skunks, mink, muskrats, and weasels, the raccoon is a distant relative of the bear. A large male can weight thirty pounds or more and is about the size of a cocker spaniel. Their front paws look like little hands, and their planigrade feet look almost like the feet of little children. Those little hands get into every crevace and crack and are used to "feel" around under water at the edges of lakes, swamps, and streams, as they look for crawfish, insect larvae, frogs, and fish. But they are omnivores and also love to raid sweet corn out of home gardens, steal bird seed from feeders, and nibble dog food left on porches and patios. They will feed on most anything, including snakes, vegetables—amost anything edible. Because of their varied diets and lack of fear of people, raccoons have moved into suburbia in a big way, making themselves at home almost anywhere, often taking shelter in holes under outbuildings and sheds right next to mowed yards and play areas. In wilder areas, they still don't want to bother making their own dens, but are very ready to take over what is available. In a study of three hundred nine raccon dens, researchers found eighty-nine in hollow trees, twenty-nine in tree nests, ninety-nine in holes among tree roots, twenty-four in rock dens, sixty-six in ground dens, and two in barns.

Raccoons have litters of three to six in the spring. By fall the kits are ready to live on their own. As a species, they are both resourceful and cunning, finding a living even in cities. They can live up to fifteen years, but because they are preyed upon by larger animals and are often victims on highways, few make it past their second year.

Raccoons do not hibernate the way bears do, but will lay up in their dens for months, while cold and snow make making a living in Minnesota hard. But should a warm spell give reprieve even in January and February, they emerge to sniff about and see what they can find to eat. Typically, they live solitary lives, but sometimes several, probably siblings, can be found sharing a den and the warmth communal living provides. Sometimes a male will band with several young females.

Because raccoons, like other desirable fur-bearing animals spend time near water, they have lush coats in the fall when their pelts are prime.

Raccoons are inquisitive, adventurous and sometimes quarrelsome amongst themselves. As youngsters, they have made interesting, fun-loving pets, but they get aggressive as they grow and cease being safe, as is true of most wild animals. Because they tolerate humans and live in close proximation to where we also live and play, they are often considered pests. They can be responsible for overturned garbage cans, spoiled gardens, and pulled down bird feeders. Their cunning can also put pets at risk, especially near water. When attacked by a dog, one of the raccoon's strategies is to jump on a dog's head in water, trying to drown it. In areas where raccoon have learned this technique, coon hunters often included airedales with the typical baying coon hound pack. The airedale doesn't bay, but when lured into water, it was not so easily tricked like the hounds and often treed the raccoon when the hounds risked being drowned.

The real threat that raccoons pose is rabies. They harbor the deadly virus and can pass it to family pets they bite or even humans. Their willingness to live close to humans puts that risk as close as the suburban back fence or even town alley.

10

Other Animals

TRAPPING IN MY YOUTH, I saw a few fox tracks but never a fox. The story of seeing my first fox and how it led me to my first deer is in my deer hunting section.

The Red Fox

The red fox is a native of North America, as it is native to many countries in the Northern Hemisphere, and it varies very little from its Asian, British, and Northern European cousins. They are very smart, cautious and elusive, and can adapt to a wide variety of environments, being almost as common in large cities (where they live on the other adaptable animals—mice, rabbits, squirrels, insects—as well as road kills, garbage, and fruit) as they are in country settings. In fact, subburbia provides foxes with ample enough habitat to make them pests.

Foxes create several dens, often enlarging groundhog or other digging animal burrows, which they use in the winter and when they have kits. They give birth in March and April and have three to seven kits in a litter, the size of the litter and the survivability of the kits dependent on the availability of food. But the fox is a most resourceful hunter, and their territory is only expanding. The size of foxes varies but averages ten to fifteen pounds in the northern states, though they can be much smaller in the south, averaging six to eight pounds.

Foxes have acute hearing, able to hear the rustle of a mouse in forest litter, and often can be seen listening, then leaping ahead, landing (even through snow) at the exact location of the mouse. They have few enemies, other than humans.

The Gray Fox

The gray fox is far less common than the red fox. A slightly smaller animal than the red fox, it is less adaptable and prefers woods, swamps, and rough, hilly terrain and is not as fond of living near humans. It is unique among the dog cousins, being able to climb trees with the agility of a cat, which gives it hunting opportunities its red fox cousin does not have. Though it has similar eating habits as the red fox—mice, other rodents, frogs, lizards, insects—its climbing ability gives it access to squirrels and birds' nests that red foxes can't possibly reach. Red foxes make their dens in rocky outcrops, at the base of clifts or under large boulders and the roots of large trees.

Coyotes

THERE WERE NO COYOTES WHEN I was on the farm. I only have seen three. One our son shot, one was sick with mange along the road, and one was seen when hunting grouse. I was walking a grouse trail when a doe crossed the trail, followed by her fawn, and then a coyote. They were running at a leisurely pace, the deer not showing fear, but the coyote could keep up the pressure until the fawn tired.

There have been occasional coyotes at my brother-in-law's farm, giving him a surprise one night. He went to a machine shed about midnight and turned on a light, startling a pack of coyotes about one-hundred feet away near a grove of trees. They began yelping and howling. He had never heard coyotes before and thought he was about to be attacked.

Working near Hinkley, Minnesota, in early spring one year, I found what I thought must be a timber wolf lying dead in the snow. It had been dead for some time and been snowed on. The brown fur had caused the snow to thaw quicker over the body and it was beautiful, framed in glistening melting snow. Thinking it might be a timber wolf, I didn't want to move it. Getting home that night, I called the game

warden and gave the location. He called back the next night and told me it was a coyote, and I could have possession of it if I wanted. I didn't want it, but I called my son Lowell and told him about it. He was interested and made the 100-mile trip to retrieve the carcus, which he planned to have mounted. Dispite having been in the snow for some time, the hide was still good. In skinning it, we found one .22-caliber shot in its lungs.

Coyotes

Coyotes, smaller than wolves but larger than red foxes, range in size from twenty to fifty pounds. They live in small family groups—a mated pair and their offspring (two to six pups)—and can hunt in that fashion, but they do not have the more complex structure of wolf societies. Youngsters grow up, go off on their own and develop their own family groups. They do howl—often in the evening to join up—but their voices are shorter, more yippy and far less dramatic than wolf voices.

Like the red fox, however, the coyotes is a master of adaptability. Even with heavy hunting pressure put on it by ranchers and sheep farmers, having been shot and poisoned and run down for over one hundred years, the coyote has steadily increased its range and moved deeper and deeper into human places. They often make a good living in cities and suburban habitats, where they live so cautiously and warily that most people don't know they are about. Though they are capable of killing sheep, especially lambs, young calves, and family pets, like the red fox, coyotes specialize in much smaller prey: rodents, rabbits, lizards, frogs, and insects.

Coyotes have a life span of about fifteen years, but typical of many species, living to adulthood is the first challenge, and only about twenty percent manage that. They are the apex predator in much of their range, but where their range overlaps with wolves, they are often persecuted by wolves or driven out.

They use dens mostly for tending to their young, but when the youngsters are mobile enough to follow their parents, dens are abandoned, and coyotes roam over a wide range. They can run up to forty miles per hour and, therefore, travel very far in a night or several days.

Beavers

IN MY YOUTH, I HAD NO OPPORTUNITY to trap beavers and it was rare even to see one.

When my son Lowell was four, we were camping in northern Minnesota and took a hike into the woods. We came to a slough that had dried up. In its center we found an abandoned beaver lodge. Lowell was able to crawl into the lodge and examine the living quarters.

Beaver

Beaver were a source of income for our early explorers and pioneers, and, in some areas, they were trapped to extinction. Beavers are the second largest rodents in the world, only topped in size by the South American capybara, although thousands of years ago a species of beaver existed in North America that was seven and one-half feet long. Having recovered from the effects of the early American fur trade, beavers are now common, sometimes pests as they change the flow of streams.

Beavers require water, living in lakes, rivers, or deep sloughs. They usually build lodges (which can often be six feet high and twice that in width) but can dig burrows into the banks of lakes and rivers. Lodges are constructed of sticks, logs, mud, and leaves. They have several underwater entrances to the den inside the lodge, the platform of which is usually four to six inches above the water line.

Besides lodges, beavers build dams, the purpose being to increase the depth of the water, to create a pond from a stream, to change a slough to a marsh. The beaver's dam can be surprisingly long and is also constructed with logs, branches and mud. A family of six can construct a thirty-five-foot dam in a week, and some dams have been measured at over 1,000 feet and have been maintained by generations of beavers. By flooding streams and raising water levels in sloughs and marshes, beavers can reach trees without traveling far from the water's edge. Trees have a dual purpose for beavers. They are used in the construction of their lodges and dams, but they are also food. Beavers live off the tender young inner bark of new growth, and to get at those new branches, trees must be felled. Beavers store food branches under water for winter use, wedging the ends of branches in the mud of their ponds. When nearby trees have been cut down, beavers will either have to move or build canals to new stands of trees. A family of beavers can clear an acre of trees (they favor aspen) in two years.

Eventually, ponds fill with silt and marshes and sloughs become meadows. When they do, because of beaver activity, they are particularly fertile land.

Beavers can stay under water for up to fifteen minutes and can swim under water for half a mile. They usually have litters of two to four kits. The babies stay with their parents until a new litter is born in the spring of the next year. At that point they are forced out. Beavers can live up to twelve years, but their mortality rate is high, especially for those yearlings newly out on their own and looking for their own water ways. Though their main enemies have been humans, when they are on land, they can fall victim to wolves, lynx, bobcats, coyotes, or dogs.

Porcupines

I HAVE ENCOUNTERED MANY PORCUPINES in the north woods and found them good to eat. How I was somehow required to eat my first porky is told in my deer-hunting section.

To dress the porkies, I begin by opening the skin on the belly and "shuck" the body out of the skin and quills. I once dressed a porky in the woods with only a pen knife.

I once took two porkies to a chuch wild game feed. It was possible that the favorite wild game that night was the lowly porcupine, and the next year people asked for more.

Porcupine

Though they have no value as a fur animal, they are most interesting, and their quills have been prized by Native Americans and put to use in many applications, including decoration. Never common, porcupines used to be protected as, it was said, if a person found himself lost in the woods and short of food, they could always catch a porcupine. As they have become rarer, only their eating proclivities have impacted what people think of them, and they have lost their protection. Porcupines eat the tender inner bark of mostly conifers, and they are responsible for the demise of many large pines. They eat twigs, buds, and leaves as well. People living in the north where the "porky" lives do not want their specimen trees killed or maimed by porcupines, forest managers hate the destruction they can cause in planted groves, and campers don't like vistas spoiled by injured trees or they pets hurt by the quills.

To many the porcupine is considered dumb, slow-moving, and destructive with a prominent defense system. They have poor vision, but have good hearing and a fine sense of smell. Their quills, some 30,000 of them, come 100 per square inch. They can't "shoot" their quills, but do back to an attacker and swing their tails, which, besides often connecting with a part of the attacker's body have a dry rattle-like sound as a warning. If the quills connect with the soft tissue of an animal's mouth, the barbs (modified scales) easily embed themselves in the flesh and come loose from the porcupine. There is instant pain, of course, but the real danger of a scuffle with a porcupine is that the quills work their way into the tissue, often making it difficult or impossible for the attacker to eat. A brush with a porcupine that does not result in death forever makes a predator reluctant to repeat the experience.

Porcupines grow to forty pounds, and despite living in trees, seldom fall. They have strong legs and feet and can hang from a limb by a single toe. Their expertise in trees includes using them as elevators, climbing to the top or out to the end of a long branch that then sags with their weight, giving them quick access to lower branches or other trees. Their enemies include humans, roadways, and fishers, that eight- to eleven-pound member of the weasel family. A fisher will attack the head, one of the few places there are no quills, then flip it over, exposing the also quill-free stomach. Foresters often relocate fishers to keep porcupine numbers in check.

Lowell chasing a porcupine.

Badgers

IN MY YOUTH, THERE WERE A FEW BADGERS around, but even at that, I saw only four or five. I've seen none in years. I tried to trap one in our pasture and thought they would be dumb and slow like skunks, especially since they have somewhat similar markings. Though not black, their grey, grizzled fur is marked by a white stripe down their backs and white and black markings on their faces. But badgers are not anything like skunks in temperament.

I placed my trap at the

entrance to the den and covered it with a bit of sand. The next morning, the entrance was quite thoroughly plugged, the trap buried, and the badger had already made a new exit hole elsewhere. It never came back to that entrance. The burying of the trap seemed more vindictive than happenstance. I took the hint.

The Badger

The badger is a good-sized member of the weasel family, and, therefore, related to skunks, martens, and otters, among others, though their temperaments are more like their "big brother" the wolverine. Typical of many weasels, badgers can have quick tempers and stick up for themselves against adversaries that easily outweigh their twelve to sixteen pounds, like bears, wolves, and coyotes. In contests with coyotes, the outcome is far from sure, with the badger often feasting on coyote as the other way around. Because of this, perhaps, the two often enjoy a kind of detente and have even been seen hunting together. With sharp teeth and powerful legs with heavy claws, they defend themselves well and are fast, powerful diggers, often outdigging pocket gophers and moles, which are also considered fast diggers. Though built close to the ground and having what seems excess flesh on their sides, making them look like moving doormats, they are no slouches when they want to put on the speed, attaining nearly twenty miles per hour in short bursts. As a result of all their digging, they have many dens and change them often except when they have young, which are born in March and number one to five.

Because badgers are consumate hole diggers, they are not liked by farmers and ranchers, who see their cows and horses breaking their legs in those holes. But, because badgers believe they can take on all comers, they easily fall victim to being shot, poisoned, gassed in their setts, and trapped and have been hunted as pests for a long time. As a result, this large member of the weasel clan has declined greatly in numbers. I haven't seen one in over thirty years.

Badgers have few enemies outside of humans, and their claws, teeth, and attitude often preclude others testing their resolve. They also, like many weasels, have an unpleasant odor.

Black Bear

GROWING UP, I HEARD ABOUT BEARS, but there were few in our area. If one was seen, it was news for the paper. When I began to deer hunt, I discovered that it was legal to shoot a bear if I had a deer license.

Jim had hunted bears around his home in northern Minnesota for over forty years, but he only shot one bear. In those years there was little bear baiting. Without baiting today, few bears would be shot.

I missed my only chance in my early years to bag a bear by not being alert. I was walking back to my car at noon during a deer hunt, when I heart a rustle at the top of a bank along the trail and then a "Whup, whup," like the sound of someone slapping his thigh with a gloved hand. A bear had apparently been watching me and had made the noise.

I would occasionally see tracks or tree scrapings made by bears. A tree with one of our stands had the claw marks of some playful cubs.

In later years I thought about hunting bear, but with a busy work schedule, the long distance to good bear country and many baits to maintain, I just didn't get that interested. But our son got the urge to hunt bears when he was in his twenties. He went to Duluth, talked to the D.N.R., who recommended his contact some homeowners north of Two Harbors as that was good bear country.

Several miles north of town, he talked to an older couple living on a narrow, dead end gravel road. They had seen bears in their yard during the summer and invited

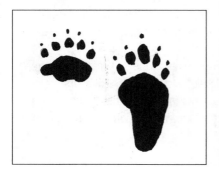

Black Bear

Our Minnesota black bear is the smallest of the North American bears, which includes the grizzly, the Kodiak, and the polar bear. There are eight species of bears worldwide with a number of subspecies. Adult female black bears typically weigh 100 to 200 pounds, with adult males coming in at 150 to 400 pounds. The largest wild black bear recorded tipped the scales at 880 pounds and was shot in North Carolina. In captivity, a male can balloon out to 950 to 1,000 pounds, and females run 555 pounds. Male bears typically roam some 200 square miles, but the range of female bears is only about thirty-five square miles.

Black bears are opportunists and omnivores, meaning they eat whatever they can find. If they stumble across a fawn, they'll kill and eat it, as they will any animal they can attack, but typically their diet is eighty-five percent vegetation, everything from grass to tubers to berries in season. They also rip apart logs for the insect life hidden there, and, yes, bears like honey. Carrion also is on the black bear's large, varied menu.

Bears tend to be loners, males keeping to themselves and females only seen in company of her current cubs. Only in the breeding season do the males and females spend time together. Females go into heat in the fall and give birth to very tiny, naked cubs in late January or early February. There are usually two cubs born at a time, though litters of six have been recorded. These newborns weigh in at ten to sixteen ounces, very tiny considering the size of the mother bear. Females usually have their first cubs when they come to maturity, usually three to five years of age.

Bears hibernate in the winter, going into their dens in October to November. Dens can be hollow trees, under roots, beneath logs or rocks, in caves or even culverts and sharp depressions. There have been records of bears hibernating above ground in cornfields, but the survivability of those individuals could be in question. Because bears are in hibernation in January and February, the cubs are born to sleepy mothers who clean them up, cuddle them close attached to a teat, and go back to sleep. The cubs see their first sunshine when the mother bear emerges in April or May.

Bears mark territory and wield silent battle with rivals by making scratched in tree bark. The higher they can scratch, surely the bigger the bear. But black bears are not a serious threat to humans. Seldom are there attacks (mostly mother bears separated from their cubs), and when attacks do occur, injuries are seldom serious.

him to hunt. With a four-hour drive coming from St. Cloud, he got to their home about noon and immediately went to look for an ambush location. With good hunting skills, he located a likely spot. But he had no stand and no pre-baiting opportunities. Instead, he spread a large circle with molasses. In about an hour, a two-year-old walked in to investigate the enticing sweetness of the molasses, and Lowell scored.

This couple had a close neighbor who offered to bait for me and showed me a good location. The neighbor built a stand, dug a pit and, cutting some logs, he had a place to bait for me. On opening day, as the sun was setting, a young bear came walking down the trail, stopping first to check out some apples I had placed on the trail. They might have looked good, but the smell of bismarks and donuts was better. It was enjoyable watching the bear toss aside the logs to get to the pastries and then devour them. It did so with clear enjoyment and little hurry.

Hoping a larger bear would come along, I waited until it was getting difficult to make out the bear in the scope. At the point when I decided it was this bear or nothing and I raised my rifle, the bear either saw or heard me and made a dash for the brush. I got off a shot but missed. I thought it might be my scope, but when I checked it out in the morning, it looked clear.

The next evening was eventful, but not in the way I had hoped. As I stood in my stand, a hawk few by less than ten feet from me. It seemed to notice me and lighted on a branch some eight feet beyond the tree with my stand, but the branch it rested on made it such that the tree's trunk blocked its view of me. The hawk would stretch itself to look around the trunk, but when I saw it, I ducked back out of its view. This hide-and-seek went on for a minute or so before the hawk flew off.

A short time later, three raccoons arrived for supper. Filled out with winter coats, they were beautiful. They couldn't move the logs, but I found it fascinating to watch them reach with their delicate hands and fingers between the logs to retrieve the pastries. That alone was worth the long drive.

That fall, after having some eye trouble during deer season, I was advised to have a cataract removed from my right eye, my shooting eye. It was during the next year that I got my first bear. I scored on the first evening with a nice 160-pound male. I was lucky. I had to work in the morning of that day until 9:00, so that I could leave for the woods only at 10:00. I got my bear early and headed for home soon after I had the animal dressed and loaded in the car, leaving at 2:30 a.m. and getting home at 6:30. It felt good to get a bear in my twenty-and-one-half-hour hunting window.

I enjoyed the hunt, but with the time constraints, I never got back to hunt again.

Grandsons Cody and Weston.

Opossum

I SAW MY FIRST OPOSSUM in the early days of 2000, but they are more common now. As they have little value to their pelts, I probably wouldn't have trapped them much as a youth anyway.

I had an experience with them, however, while helping my brother-in-law pick corn in early November one year. I noticed a small piece of corn husk moving slowly along the ground near the barn. The fact that it was moving against the wind made me want to investigate. What I found surprised me. A tiny opossum was carrying food to its shelter. The baby was about the size of a large mouse, but it looked larger with its bristly gray fur.

We later saw the mother opossum and two young near the hay, but I have no information if they survived the winter or not.

The marsupials have very short lives compared to placental mammals their size, living maybe two years in this area due to severe winters, predators, and traffic, but in captivity they live five to ten years.

65

Opossum

The opossum is the only naturally occuring marsupial in North America, although they used to outnumber placental mammals in both North and South America. Many species died out from both continents, though a number still inhabit South America. Only the Virginia Opossum remains in the north. Much more prevalent in the southern states, the range of the "possum" has been steadily widening as the species gradually makes its way north.

The opossum is not a large animal, though it stands about mid-range for marsupials, being about the size of a cat to not quite as large as female raccoon. Males are generally the larger individuals. Because they are marsupials, that is they carry their young in a pounch on the belly, and because they can have more than one litter a year (usually two), their breeding period is wide, ranging from December to March, and then spring to early summer. Marsupials have short gestations, and the opossum's is only thirteen days. The babies are born at a very early stage of development, having mostly forelegs and a well-developed mouth. They are blind and naked at birth. The mother produces surprisingly large litters, from seventeen to twenty-one babies, but these tiny little creatures must travel from the vagina up the belly to the pouch, crawl inside and find a teat, to which they latch on (to the point that they fuse with the teat), where they remain for the next fifty-five to sixty days. The problem is that momma opossum only had a dozen to thirteen teats. It's first come, first served for those tiny babies.

Opossums use woodchuck burrows for their dens, as well as hollow trees, brush piles, culverts, and buildings. They forage at night, living on a diet of worms, insects, bird eggs, small mammals, snakes, fruit, and nuts. They are not opposed to carrion either, which, unfortunately accounts for many deaths on roadways.

They are typically solitary individuals, coming together mostly for breeding. They tend to change dens frequently and are wanderers without defined territories. In areas with high populations, dens stand at least 1,000 feet apart and the individuals roam up to 2,000 feet from those dens.

Opossums are slow-moving creatures with few defenses. They hiss and growl, showing their fifty teeth, but often "play possum," when threatened, holding still, leaving their mouth slightly open and not moving for a few minutes to hours. It can save their lives, but it can as often allow a fox or coyote time to snatch them up with ease. Their scaly, mostly naked tails are prehensile and helps them stabilize themselves in trees, but they can't (not adults at least) hang from those tails, though youngsters can briefly.

Part Two

Bird Hunting

11

Duck Hunting

Moving to our new farm, with our house only 100 feet from the large slough was exciting, but I didn't realize its true value until September 19, 1944.

That Tuesday afternoon, cars pulling boats began arriving in our yard, and the men talked to each other like it was a family reunion.

I didn't know there was a duck season until that day, and Florida Sloughs were a duck-hunter's paradise.

The hunters were all from the Minneapolis area and had hunted here for years. They started coming the day before duck season opened to check out the slough and locate their duck blinds for the opening morning. Since the season opened half an hour before sunrise, that was no time to be setting things up.

The men had hunted together for many years, and each knew the area he wanted to hunt. The others knew, too, and respected each other's location.

It was exciting for me as I helped carry their duck boats to the shore and watched as they rowed out to locate their blinds.

It was a large slough, with much of it over four feet deep with enough cattails and reeds to camouflage a hunter in only a few areas.

I Felt Needed

COMING BACK TO SHORE, THE MEN ASKED me for some wild hay as they prepared their boats for the morning hunt. They wanted the hay in the bottoms of their boats to help camouflage the boats from above with its green and brown color. It also deadened the sounds made from moving about in a boat and kept things from bumping into each other if the boat rocked with water action. Several hunters shared a bale of hay, and each gave me a quarter.

With the hay in the boats, they began bringing bags of wooden ducks. I had never seen or heard of wooden ducks and was intrigued at what they were going to do with them. Surely this was not some game: hunters go out and bring back wooden ducks.

A few years before this, live ducks were used for decoying. Hunters would take two or more tame ducks, the noisier the better, tether them by rings around their necks connected to a line and anchor and have them swim near their blinds. This worked rather well, possibly better than wood ducks, which is probably why hunters developed duck calls.

With their boats prepared, the hunters chatted and then left to stay with friends or at a nearby hotel.

I had a restless night, excited for the action to begin the next morning. I woke at 4:00 a.m. at the sound of the first car pulling into our yard. By 4:30, there were seven cars, including two that had not been there the previous day. The new hunters had scouted the lake earlier in the week and knew their destinations. They had asked for hay.

I had never been to the shore before sunrise, and it was interesting to listen to the night sounds of hundreds of ducks out on the slough.

I enjoyed watching the boats launch, quickly and quietly disappearing into the darkness with the only sound being the dip and splash of their oars. I wondered how they could all find their way in the dark.

As the boats disappeared, the ducks began to get nervous. I could hear the difference in their calls. Some of the older ducks had been through this experience before. Some rafts of ducks took flight, and I could hear the whistling of their wings and even see what looked like small clouds against the pale eastern sky.

As the hunters reached their blinds, the rowing sounds ceased. Then I could hear some splashing as they threw out their wooden ducks, and some boat sounds as they settled into hunting positions and arranged their boats. The last sounds were the clanking of metal as they loaded their shotguns.

All the experienced hunters knew the exact time of the opening, down to the minute it seemed. One half hour before sunrise. Having no watch, I often wondered why they weren't shooting, as there were many ducks flying around. As the dawn neared and I could see some of the decoys out on the slough, I also saw some ducks landing amongst the wooden birds. Still the men didn't shoot. The sky warmed in the east.

Suddenly, it was as if the slough erupted all at once. Shots came from many quarters all over the slough, and the air was filled with the whistling wings of many species of ducks. I saw a duck fall, then, a split-second later, I heard the shot. Then the whole slough became a battle-field. Hunters were shooting, ducks by the hundreds were flying around in mad confusion, squawking and quacking madly. It was bedlam.

Some flights of ducks quickly left the slough, but hunting had begun all over the area, and other flights soon came skating in, looking for santuary from other hunters on other sloughs and lakes.

As I watched the scene, I would often see two or three crumple and fall out of the sky, again followed just a split second later by the shots that had killed them. (The hunters later explained that it took a split second for the sound to reach me on shore, though I could instantly see the birds fall.)

I had to leave on a two-mile walk to our country school, but I was anxious to get back that evening. I was home well before sunset, the close of shooting for the day, but several boats had already come in, having reached their limit of ten ducks.

I had never seen a wild duck up close, and the hunters showed me the different species and the differences between males and females in the species. I was impressed by the beautiful plumage, especially in the more colorful males. Most of the hen ducks were drab in color to provide camouflage when sitting on their eggs.

From what I saw, the hunters favored the green-headed drake mallards. Those seemed to be their prime target. They were the largest of the ducks in the area, and, in flight, they could easily see which were the males and which the females. These were the ducks of pride. Those and the blue and green-winged teal were the most abundant, but they also showed me a few redheads, pintails, canvasbacks, and ruddy ducks.

Another common duck out on the slough, but not popular with the hunters was the spoonbill. The name comes from the shape of the duck's bill, which was long and wide at the end, shaped like a spoon. The hunters explained that it was a bottom feeder, the "spoon" being used to advantage as it scavenged the slough bottom for insect larva and other food. But the hunters said they weren't the best tasting of ducks. They were seldom shot because, within shotgun range, even though they had a green head like the mallard, their big spoon bill was easily recognized. Though in a drabber plumage in the fall than during the breeding season, this was one of the more colorful ducks in their spring plumage.

With a mid-week opener for duck season, many of the hunters had jobs, and they needed to head home that night, saying they would be back on Saturday.

After the excitement of the morning, I was eager for a repeat on Saturday morning when I could be home all day.

Before the hunters left, they cleaned out their boats, leaving the hay on shore. Herman asked me to collect the hay to feed to the horses. I did so, finding many expended shotgun shells in the process. And also a few live ones.

I met the hunters when they returned early Saturday morning, and I had a bale of hay ready for them. As I didn't have school, I watched them launch, then ran to a hill in our pasture that overlooked the slough. I wanted to see all the action. The land was flat for several hundred yards around the slough, but then rose sharply into our pasture hill, as part of the glacieral ridge. It was in the northeast corner of our pasture.

From my raised location, I could see the blinds and even recognize some of the hunters. I was surprised at the large number of ducks flying overhead, both leaving and entering the slough. As there were several lakes and sloughs to our southeast, I figured the birds routinely flew between them. The ducks would often be low as they came off the slough, then gradually rise as they approached the hill. The ducks coming into the slough flew over much higher. There was no natural cover in the pasture, but on cloudy or rainy morinngs, the hilltop could provide great shooting as the ducks few lower coming in. In the early morning, I would often hear their wings before they were actually visible. Some times, really early in the morning, I only heard the wings and never saw the birds themselves. When I started hunting ducks in the early morning, especially those dark mornings, I could aim at the wing whistle, shoot and wait for the *thump* to to tell me I had hit my target.

I really enjoyed watching the flights of ducks circle the slough, and I often wondered why the hunters didn't shoot at ducks that looked close enough.

That Saturday, the hunting wasn't as good or dramatic as on the opener, but the hunters seemed satisfied nonetheless, and most planned on coming back and hunting on Sunday. Two hunters even stayed in a tent in our yard, while the others left for motels or friends' houses and returned the next morning.

Wall of Fame

EITHER WAY, IT WAS IMPORTANT to the hunters to cool off their ducks to avoid spoilage. They did this by hanging the birds in our corn crib. How they did even this intrigued me. They inserted the birds' bills through the gaps in the wall of the corn crib from the inside so the bills stuck out and held the birds in place. By spacing them along the wall, the birds had good air circulation, and our cool September nights provided proper cooling.

With often ten or more hunters, there were many rows of ducks in our corn crib, all lined up by size and species. The hunter with the largest number of ducks always had bragging rights, as well as the hunter with the greatest number of green heads (mallards).

I enjoyed inspecting the ducks in the corn crib, looking at the beautiful plumage and study where the birds had been hit. When I found a strange duck I didn't know, I'd ask the hunters about it.

When the boats left again on Sunday evening, I again gathered up the hay for use in the barn and found more spent and live shells.

Most hunters said they wouldn't be back the next weekend, but they asked Mother about room and board for the next season. I was excited, as was Mother, as this would mean some income, more than the quarters I collected for the hay. As hunting in the slough had already gone on for years, we felt we couldn't charge for parking on our property, launching off our shore or hunting on our land. But we could charge for two beds, mine and my sister's, and a cot.

They agreed to $3.00 for a bed, seventy-five cents for breakfast and one dollar for supper. Other hunters not staying with us wanted meals too, and that meant more income. Before leaving, most of the hunters gave me either a candy bar they had left over as a snack out on the slough or a quarter.

That fall, as I was looking for places to trap, I walked along the east shore, which was the neighbor's pasture, to a large point at the northeast corner of the slough. The point extended about a third of a mile to the west. It was also a pasture with little cover for duck hunters, but it was a place where I could hunt ducks.

The next year, some hunters came up the evening before the season opened to stay in the house with two other hunters staying in a tent. They wanted the meal portion of the agreement, though.

Midnight Visitor

Tex was one of my two favorite hunters, and Kent the other one, both of whom were staying at the house.

The next morning, the two hunters who had stayed in a tent told of a strange experience they had had. When they got up in the morning, they discovered that some meat in a box of groceries they had brought along had been half eaten, and they were sure it hadn't been a mouse.

Tex immediately said it was a skunk. They said it couldn't have been a skunk because there was a floor to the tent they had used, and both entry flaps had been tied shut.

The morning of the second day, when they came in for breakfast they told Tex he had been correct. Their meat thief was a skunk. During the night, one of the hunters was awakened by a noise in the food box. When he opened his eyes, he found himself nose to nose with a skunk, a very fat one. Nudging his buddy, he said, "Wake up but don't move. We have company in the tent."

Hearing them whisper, the skunk grabbed a box of cookies and slid between the canvas flaps. They found the torn apart box and half the cookies eaten in the morning. It lay just a short distance from the tent.

On Sunday, I walked along the east shore, heading to the point to watch some of the action. The pasture on the east side of the slough was grazed all the way to the water's edge, but there were a couple areas where some weeds stood at the shore. From one of these areas, a mallard duck struggled to swim out into the slough. A short distance farther, I found feathers where a duck had been eaten by an animal. Then I saw a dead teal floating in the water. It appeared fresh, probably from the day before. I took it home and showed it to Tex. He pronounced it fresh enough to eat. He showed me that, by examining a duck's eyes, I could decide the condition of the meat, if it was fresh enough to eat or had been floating several days.

Tex also explained the duck on shore. Many ducks, he told me, were wounded in the hunting. Some would die, while others held on for some time. With the northwesterly or west wind, both the wounded and dead not found or that had died later were blown toward the east shore. Predators there certainly wouldn't turn down such a meal handed to them.

I realized I could bring home ducks to eat by frequenting that east shore. Going out on Monday evening, I did indeed find another dead mallard, but by the eyes I knew it didn't appear fresh enough to eat. Some birds that actually died on Saturday but had not been recovered by the hunters might take longer to be blown to that east shore. This bird didn't appear to be a Sunday kill.

The next weekend, most of the hunters were back, and when my parents left on Sunday afternoon, I decided to take Herman's twelve-gauge, double-barreled shotgun and look for shore ducks. I had never shot the shotgun, but I had some shells.

Walking to the shore, I found a dead teal, still fresh, and an injured mallard struggling out from the shore. After picking up the teal and mallard, I went out to the point to watch the action. It was a warm, sunny day with few ducks flying, so I lay in the pasture, waiting for the hunters to do something, or occasionally I sat up to watch for flying ducks. From behind me, a green-headed mallard winged toward me, but it was very high. I had listened carefully to the hunters at supper, how they had to lead the point of their barrel well ahead of the flying birds so the shot caught up with them when they reached the place they aimed. This distance was based on wind speed, the height of the bird, the speed, even the fact that a larger bird looked slower than a smaller one . . . a lot of factors.

Never Again

I LAY ON MY BACK, WAITING FOR THE MALLARD to get overhead. I took long careful aim and fired. To my absolute surprise, the bird folded. I had hit it! But at its height and with a strong tail wind, it landed well out in the slough and began to drift even further out.

I was excited to have hit the first bird I aimed at, but dismayed to see it getting further away every moment. I was afraid I was going to lose it and it would be wasted. But it was drifting toward some of the hunters. I hoped they'd pick it up because wasting the meat bothered me more than losing the bird.

As my excitement lessened, I began to notice a sharp pain in my right shoulder. I learned that it was not wise to shoot a shotgun while lying on my back.

I got back before my folks arrived back home and put the gun back in the closet.

That evening one of the hunters showed off a big green head and was telling us about what a great shot someone had made. Other hunters had also seen the mallard hit high up and fall into the slough.

I was too embarrassed to say I had made that shot, and I couldn't let my parents know because I wasn't supposed to take the gun out.

That year, 1945, the season ended on December 8th.

Ducks on Ice

On the last weekend of the season, most of the lakes and sloughs were frozen over, but there was a heavy migration of northern ducks and geese that continued to move through.

Mid-morning of that last day, two hunters with a duck boat on their car stopped alongside the slough and were watching several hundred mallards circling and landing in a small area of open water near the point. We had had several days of severe cold, but also some days with heavy duck migration. The ducks had been using the slough as an evening rest over, and the constant action of hundreds of ducks had kept the water open. I had noticed the area was always the last to freeze up. I thought maybe a spring fed into the slough about there.

The hunters checked the ice near the shore, and it easily supported their weight. But it was about half a mile to the ducks. Still, they couldn't resist the opportunity. They off-loaded their duck boat and carried it to the edge of the ice, along with two bags of decoys. They started out. With a flat-bottomed boat, it helped support their weight and could be pushed over the ice pretty easily.

I watched for a few minutes as they made slow, careful progress, and then went to the barn. Well over an hour later, I began to hear some

Duck hunters pulled their boat across the ice to get to their duck-hunting location.

steady shooting. I went to the shore and saw many ducks circling the slough with a few new flocks coming in, all wanting to land in the open water.

By late afternoon, I heard the boat scraping on the ice again and went down to meet the hunters. They were exhausted but very excited, as they laid out nineteen mallards, seventeen of which were drakes. They said they had left two on the ice as they were too difficult to retrieve.

They said the ice was solid to very near the open water. They had gone into the water and thrown in their decoys from there. The difficulty was getting back onto the ice after retrieving their decoys and the ducks that had hit the water. Some of the downed ducks had landed on thin ice at the water's edge, and they just couldn't get to them.

That was the last year with a ten birds per hunter and twenty per person limit. In 1946 it was reduced to seven and fourteen.

My Own Gun

I BELIEVE HERMAN KNEW I WAS USING HIS SHOTGUN, because the next year he bought me a new J.C. Heggens (Sears), twelve-gauge, pump-action shotgun. It was much lighter than his and fit me perfectly. With some practice on blackbirds in the summer, I was gaining confidence by duck-hunting season.

I continued looking for ducks along the shore and could now hunt the hill and the small sloughs behind the hills. Soon I was bringing back more ducks than Mother wanted, so I would sell some of my ducks to the hunters for three shells each. That kept me in ammunition.

I also becan searching the south shore for dead ducks, but with the woods and the brush, they were hard to spot, and wounded ducks could easily hide.

My first duck in flight taken with my new gun was when a flight of six mallards came over. I aimed at the lead duck, but the third one dropped. That gave me another lesson in judging the lead distance I had to use to hit my target.

My best luck came jump shooting ducks as they raised off the small sloughs. They were moving more slowly and usually straight away. No lead was needed.

Hunting the sloughs from 1944 to 1952, I never saw a hunter bring in a goose, but I saw thousands of them as they made their southward migration. In those years, we were on the northern duck and goose main migration route and would sometimes see many single flocks strung out well over a mile.

Concerned Geese

DURING THE FALL MIGRATION, I heard a flock that seemed closer and noisier than most, and they were circling the point.

Going to the shore, I saw about twenty-five geese circling a small area of water. They flew back and forth over that area. A goose on the water appeared to be injured and a goose flew on either side of the

injured one, trying to help it lift off the water. After several attempts, they rose and joined the flock to continue south, but two more geese flew down to assist the one on the water. After several more unsuccessful tries, these geese also rose to the main flock. During all this was constant chatter between the geese, the one on the water, the helpers, and the others circling above them.

Finally, the flock must have felt they could wait no longer and headed out, leaving the goose on the water behind. Long after their voices faded with distance, I could hear the frantic calls of the lone goose.

I called the game warden, and he said he'd come out the next day. He didn't come, though, probably knowing there was little to be done.

Walking to the point the next morning, I looked for the lone goose in the area where it had been, but there was no sign of it. I assumed its calling had attracted one of our numerous predators, a mink or a fox.

It was past hunting season, and I assumed the goose had been injured during the season and was forced, by weakness or difficulty flying, to leave the flock.

Surprised Teacher

In 1950, the duck season started at noon on Friday, and those wanting to hunt from my class in school could get a pass from our teacher to get off at 10:00 a.m. I never heard of a pass request being refused, but some teachers said, "Bring me a duck." I never saw that happen. Except for our choir teacher, Doris Larson, I wouldn't have brought a duck to a teacher. Doris was young, vibrant and always upbeat. She never walked into the choir room; she bounced in and was loved by all the choir members.

On Monday morning, I went on the hill at dawn and was lucky enough to shoot a beautiful adult green-head mallard. After some "fixing,"

I put the duck in a paper grocery bag and took it to school. Getting to the choir room early, to set up my joke while Doris was in her office, I laid her metal music stand flat. Removing the music, I laid the duck on the stand, belly up, with the head hanging over one side and the tail over the other. Then I spread the music so the duck was mostly hidden under it.

As the choir members came in, they were excited and could see the duck's head and tail on the stand, but I told them not to tell who had

put the duck there. Doris bounced in, the choir members were all in place, but there was an unusual hush to the room. Doris gave us her plans for the day. As she raised her baton to begin, laughter broke out. With the sloped stand, Doris had yet to see the duck. She didn't know why we were laughing and lowered her baton. The choir quieted down, and she raised the baton again. Greater laughter ensued. As she stepped back, and with the choir staring at the music stand, she noticed the duck's head hanging over the side. Raising the sheet music with a delicate thumb and finger, she fully exposed the duck. The look on her face made the choir roll with laughter.

She recovered quickly and asked who had given her the gift. Getting no reply, she gingerly grasped the duck by its feet and carried it into her office. After about fifteen minutes, we all got down to work.

Later in the day, a few minutes before the close of the school day, there was a message on the PA system for Bob Erickson to report to the choir room. Usually such requests never boded well for the student. When I arrived in the choir room, Doris said one of the students had told her I brought the duck, and she thanked me. Two days later she again called me into her office. She told me she had taken the duck to a lady who processed wild game. That woman had told Doris it was the strangest duck she had ever seen. It had no intestines, but it did have a note in the body cavity. I acted surprised, and she again thanked me for the gift.

And Now the Rest of the Story

It wasn't until my class's fiftieth reunion in 2001 that, people who had known about the duck in the choir learned "the rest of the story." I knew it was important that, unless a person was processing a duck soon, it had to be cleaned out to maintain eating quality. Tex, however, had shown me a good method to keep that good eating quality and the moistness of the meat but still clean it out. He showed me that if I took a small branch, a little larger than a pencil in diameter and cut deep

83

notches on one end, and then inserted it up the duck's rectum, I could hook all the intestines and pull them out. They would usually break off at the gizzard, but take out all the rest of the digestive tract, which was the source of a lot of food contamination and body heat. I had done this with the mallard I gave Doris. Plus, I had inserted the note rolled up in pretty much the same way. I remember writing some crazy kid stuff in that note, but ended with "Last words: Quack Quack."

As I read this story at the reunion, the place erupted in laughter, with many recalling that day fifty years earlier.

Gotcha

I PLAYED ANOTHER JOKE WITH A SPOON-BILLED DUCK, shot by mistake and left by a hunter. My Uncle Chester from Minneapolis would bring his father up to hunt once or twice a year. They had no boat, so they would sit on the hill or on the point. They would always come up in good weather, and it was more of an outing than a serious hunt, and they got few ducks.

Coming back from the point early one afternoon, with no ducks, they went into the house where Mother always had coffee and cookies ready for them.

I had picked a spoonbill, shot by mistake, and decided to make a joke of it. I broke off a long stick with a "Y" on the end, used the hunter's boat. I laid the duck in the water about sixty feet from the front of the house in a small patch of weeds and propped up its head with that stick. Rushing into the kitchen, I told Chester a duck was near shore by the big oak. He and his dad rushed out, grabbing their guns from the porch. They hoofed it down to the lake shore.

Chester's dad was a little ahead, and Chester whispered, "Wait for me!"

I don't know who shot first, but after five shots, the duck's head was still up, and they stopped as they heard me laughing.

They proudly took the spoonbill home, but I can't imagine the number of pellets they had to spit out.

Ignorance in Youth

Kᴇɴᴛ ᴡᴀs ᴜᴘ ᴡɪᴛʜ ᴀ ꜰʀɪᴇɴᴅ ᴏɴ ᴛʜᴇ ᴡᴇᴇᴋᴇɴᴅ, and both hunted the morning in separate boats. It was a sunny day, with little wind and few other hunters to move the ducks. There were a large number of ducks on the slough, though, just far out, lounging in the open water.

At noon, Kent asked if I would chase up some ducks if he gave me his small duck boat. He also offered to let me use his wife's twenty-gauge pump shotgun and shells. This would be my first experience hunting ducks in a boat, and it was a neat, expensive gun.

He and his friend went into their two-man boat and gave me use of his one-man boat. It was like a fat canoe with a hole near the front and back through which poles could be pushed to anchor the boat in the mud.

Kent told me where they would be hunting and where to go to scare up the ducks. This was legal at that time. He said to wait half an hour for them to get into position. After that, I shoved off. In order to paddle the boat, I had the gun lying at my side, aimed ahead and ready for a quick pick up should I see ducks.

85

Raising the first flight, red heads, one duck separated from the flock and flew directly at me about thirty yards in the air. I got my first shot off at about a forty-five-degree angle, and my third shot as I leaned back to shoot over my shoulder. It dropped, and I had my first red head.

Moving around the slough, I jumped many ducks and was fortunate many flew within range. I managed to get two pintails and a ruddy duck. But most of the ducks would circle back towards the open water, staying away from the cattails . . . and the hunters. Still, I heard them shoot a few times.

After about two hours, the ducks were nervous. Many flights chose to leave the slough, so I headed for shore.

When I came back to meet up with Ken and his friend, they had only one duck to show for the time, and I gave them the two pintails. They were pleased I got the ducks. They hadn't expected that I would get any shooting. The canoe was meant to be anchored by its poles before shooting started and wasn't actually safe for open water hunting. I was fortunate I hadn't tipped it and been forced to swim back to shore, something particularly difficult wearing hunting gear, and I couldn't swim.

Dive and Hang On

I HAD SOME INTERESTING EXPERIENCES with my cousin Wayne, Chester's son. We were hunting a small slough in the hills one time. The slough had about 100 feet of open water surrounded by tall cattails. We could hear ducks in the water but had to figure out how to get to them. We each positioned ourselves at a corner of the slough and started yelling. Sure enough, that scared the birds into flight.

Wayne dropped a drake in the weeds, and I dropped a hen in the water, but mine was out of sight. Plodding through the rushes, I saw no sign of the hen. There weren't enough rushes in the middle for cover, but she stayed out of sight. I began wading across the slough, expecting the bird had swum into the weeds on the opposite shore. Nearing that shore, I heard a *plop* in the water behind me and some commotion.

86

The hen was lying belly up, with her bill grasping a reed below the surface, her feet paddling, trying to get back under the water. This was my first experience with a crippled duck diving and holding onto weeds to keep from being discovered. I've heard of them actually drowning, still locked onto their submerged weed stalk. This behavior seemed to be more common with smaller ducks, like the teal, as they had less bouyancy.

It was apparent the duck's grip had slipped, and the hen had floated to the surface. If that hadn't happened, I would have believed she had completely disappeared.

A Little Early

ONE WEEKEND, A GOOD FRIEND FROM MINNEAPOLIS had come up with a hunting friend. They hunted in the boat together on Saturday. On Sunday, the friend said he wanted to hunt on shore near the point and was let out there. When my friend came to shore, he expected to see his friend, assuming he would walk back along the shore. But no friend.

It was getting dark, and my friend came to the house, concerned that his buddy wasn't back. We knew there was no way he could get lost and suggested we wait another half hour before taking flashlights out to look for him. We waited, but no buddy.

As we were about to leave to look for him, we heard a knock on the door. It was the "lost" friend, looking tired and sweaty, but, even though we asked, he wouldn't tell us what had happened to him.

The two packed up their gear, and, as they left, the buddy asked that they turn right out of the driveway towards the southeast corner of the slough not the main road. He said, "We have to pick up a deer."

Apparently, on Saturday morning as they went out, they had seen a large buck walking along the shore near the point. The buddy had asked to hunt on shore near the point on Sunday afternoon, intending to shoot the deer even though it was a long ways from deer season. That ended the friendship between the two, but my friend learned later that his ex-buddy went on to work for the FBI.

Losing My Dream

In 1952 my parents moved to a farm near Paynesville, about fifty miles to the northeast of our old farm. It was a dramatic change in terrain, being flat land with little wildlife.

I attended school and then worked in Minneapolis, but I would come home on weekends, though I could enjoy little trapping or hunting there.

In 1962, my wife, our daughter, and I moved to St. Cloud, and I began hunting, but now I looked mostly for pheasants, grouse, and deer. In 1975, while having lunch in a restaurant, I began talking hunting with a farmer who lived thirty miles west of St. Cloud. I mentioned how much I had enjoyed duck hunting as a boy, and he told me he had a great duck-hunting slough. My interest perked up as he describes the duck slough. It was about a mile long, north to south, and about a quarter mile wide, with most of the shore lined in marsh reeds and cattails. His farm lay at the north end of the slough.

I found myself telling him I'd be interested in hunting ducks. The season was just two weeks away, and he invited me to come up for the opener. Knowing I'd probably want to look over the slough in advance to plan where I needed to put my blind, he suggested I come out during the week. He said, "Come out just before sunset, and bring your gun."

A Little Early!

I arrived at the farm with the farmer and his son eager to show me their slough, shotguns in hand. He said that, every evening about dusk, most of the ducks would leave the slough, with many flying over the barn only 200 feet from the shore. They would return at dawn.

We walked to the slough, waiting for the flocks to leave. As it wasn't duck season yet, I didn't want to shoot, but I didn't want to offend the man and spoil a good chance on the opener.

It was getting dark, with no ducks anywhere, and he seemed to be getting nervous that he had described something that wasn't going to happen that evening. But, a short time later, a large flock of about thirty green-wing teal appeared over the tall cattails, coming directly towards us and only about thirty feet in the air.

I didn't shoot, but the farmer and his son took three shots and dropped five ducks. They appeared to have done this before and were upset that I hadn't shot.

As I scouted the slough, I saw that there were few areas of cover near the center, and those areas were leased by hunters from past years. I would have to go in through a marsh and cattails and hunt near the shore. The slough looked better than Florida Sloughs, but it was surrounded by farmland and controlled by local hunters. Still I wanted to give it a try.

On opening day, I had to drag my duck boat through a hundred feet of cattails and marsh to get to the water. Setting up in the rushes, I only got a few shots off and no ducks, but the longtime hunters had great luck. I did locate where I would be the next season.

Lowell's First Hunt

THAT NEXT YEAR, I BOUGHT MY SON, LOWELL, age eleven, on his first duck hunt. I got a couple of ducks, and he maybe hit one, but we didn't see it fall, so it didn't count.

The next opener, we went out and pulled the boat into the cattails on the north end of the slough. Being in high cattails, it was difficult to see low-flying birds, forcing us to stand. Lowell, being shorter, couldn't see some of the ducks until they were in the open area in front of us. With our boat parallel to the slough and Lowell on my right, I explained how we would hunt.

If a duck came from the right, he would not shoot at the first duck but at one of the trailing ones. If they came from the left, he'd shoot at the leading duck, and I'd try for a trailing one.

Early in the morning, a single wood duck came in low from the left. It was difficult to see, but I dropped it on a quick shot. We then had some real excitement, watching the other hunters drop numerous birds and waited for our chance.

Two blue-winged teal came in from the right, flying about thirty yards out from the cattails and fifteen feet over the water. They were difficult to see, especially for Lowell, so that, by the time he could see them, he had little time to get ready. As the first duck flew in, I could see Lowell aiming at it. He apparently hadn't seen the second duck about twenty feet behind the leader. The cattails blocked his view.

I swung on the second duck, and, as I fired, I could see both ducks fall, hitting the water only a split second apart. We had shot at the same moment, so that I hadn't even heard his shot and he hadn't heard mine.

I congratulated Lowell on his first duck, but he was solemn, thinking he had missed, and I had hit his bird. I knew better. Then I realized he hadn't seen the second duck fall. We immediately went to retrieve the downed birds. Only when we picked up the second bird just twenty feet from the first did Lowell get excited at having taken his first duck.

Ironically, he shot his first pheasant nearly identically . . . but that's a story for later.

My Greatest Shots

As IT WAS SO DIFFICULT TO GET THROUGH the marsh and cattails, I only hunted that slough a few more times. On one trip I invited my fishing buddy Ron to go with me, and he brought his boat and two of his young children.

Our blinds were about fifty yards apart, with Ron and kids to the east. We had seen some ducks, but had not had a chance to shoot when I heard the sound of geese to the north. The birds were coming towards us from over the farm, but they were very high.

I quickly switched from #4 shot to B-B shot, hoping they would come within range. They flew over, well out of range, but, when I looked to my left, I saw two geen-winged teal winging in from the west, directly at me and almost upon me.

I took a quick shot as they were nearly overhead, and one dropped. I swung on the second bird, and it also dropped. Hearing a splash near the boat, I quickly looked back. The first duck had dropped only four feet from the boat. It was only crippled, though, and, seeing me, it recovered from its shock. It dove, grabbed a weed and held on out of sight. As this was happening, I heard Ron yell, "You got us full of guts!" Then I realized what I had done.

A teal is about the size of a man's hand, but, because of the geese, I had loaded my gun with heavier shot, with many less BBs and hit the second bird directly. With the goose load, nine BBs went entirely through the little bird, showering Ron and his kids with meat fragments, blood, and guts. Oh, well.

I turned my attention back to the crippled bird. With an oar, I probed the reeds where the duck had dived, and the bird popped back up to the surface where I could grab it.

Lonely

ONE WARM SUNNY DAY, I took our daughter Lynae and her friend duck hunting. I didn't expect any ducks, but they would enjoy the experience.

There were few ducks in the air and none near us. The girls talked and played in the boat. I had no decoys, but I did have a duck call, but I had never called a duck before. Hearing a lone duck calling from across the slough, I decided to answer and see if I could lure it in. After a few calls, all was silent. After a few seconds, I saw what looked like a football with wings coming at me at eye level. It was an apparently lonely green head, looking for company. How could I miss.

12

Pheasants

THERE WAS AN ABUNDANCE OF PHEASANTS on the farms where we lived, but having no one to take me hunting, I only began hunting pheasants after getting my twelve-gauge pump shotgun.

The shotgun opened new hunting experiences for me, as I could now go after the birds and not rely on them to come to me.

I don't recall my first pheasant, but it was probably from a slough near the farm. In the 1940s and early 1950s, nearly every farm field had a slough, and most of them were dry in the fall during the pheasant season. With at least six good pheasant sloughs within a ten-minute walk, I could hunt during any short break I had during the day.

After hunting ducks, I was amazed how easy it was to shoot pheasants. They usually got up close, flew slowly, and usually straight away. With few hunters, and very few with dogs, most pheasants hadn't been harrassed. When the duck hunters learned I was hunting pheasants, they became interested. In 1947 the duck opener changed from half an hour before sunrise to noon on the first day. As the hunters waited for noon, they decided to practice by shooting some trap and invited me to join them. There were six of us and we each had five shots. I hit four out of five, as did one of the other hunters. The others hit less.

The hunters were back the next weekend when pheasant season opened and asked if I could take them out pheasant hunting at noon on Sunday, after duck hunting in the morning. I thought this would be exciting. It was the first time someone had respected me to lead them. Coming in before noon, we prepared for the hunt, which would all be in the dried sloughs. I tried to organize a hunt through the weeds and brush, but they liked to let me be the brush-buster as they walked along in the shorter grass next to the slough. Being in the heavier cover and considering the way pheasants took off, I usually had the best action and first shot. I had learned to shoot fast, and most of my shots with pheasants were straight away. I seldom missed. Unfortunately I also tended to blow many birds apart.

By 3:00, the hunters were ready to head back for the evening duck shooting. We had five pheasants, and I had shot four of them. I gave them all but one, but I didn't like doing it. My family didn't have much.

They mentioned doing it again at noon the next weekend. I took my gun and went up on the hill about 11:15 and watched them come in. I then went hunting by myself.

No Nose

OUR DOG, SHEP, WAS A GOOD CATTLE DOG, and he always would go hunting with me, but he didn't have a nose for pheasants, although he was pretty good at beating the brush. He probably jumped as many skunks as pheasants, and, unfortunately usually got the worst end of of each encounter. But he would chase down crippled pheasants when he could see them and saved me several that would have escaped otherwise.

One day we brought home three pheasants and a rabbit. I put them in the porch as I went in for dinner. Shep knew how to open the screen door. I heard it slam and immediately went to check it out . . . just in time to see Shep take off with one of the pheasants. We chased him down and got that bird back only to discover that he had already been in the porch and lifted another bird. That one we never found.

.22 Marksmen

LIVING NEAR MAMRE LAKE WERE TWO RUDEEN BROTHERS who were experts with a .22 and other rifles. When hunting in a group going after pheasants, they would often take their .22s along. When others missed a bird or it was out of shotgun range, Rudeen could bring the bird down with that keen eye of his and his .22. He would also stop the escape of wing-shot cripples that could still run like mad.

Outsmarting 'Em

WHEN HUNTING ALONE, IF I DROPPED A CRIPPLE, I would quickly run up to where it had fallen, stop, and be still. Typically, when a bird first drops, it's confused, in shock. I didn't want to give it time to gather its thoughts. At the sound of the hunter approaching, many birds will freeze. After about a minute, I would slowly walk the area and usually flush the bird, sometimes by almost falling on it. With a hunting party, I would have one or two hunters stop and mark the spot where it fell, wait and then search.

On one pheasant, I marked the spot and four hunters rushed in and thoroughly searched the area. We were in some heavy cane weeds at the time. As we were about to leave, having not found the bird, I asked one of them to hold my gun. I got down on my hands and knees and crawled slowly, parting the cane as I went. Within about twenty seconds I spotted the rooster, hunkered down. We had walked within inches of it and it had held. We surrounded the bird and caught it like a barnyard chicken, without firing a shot.

Another time I was by the shore of the slough when I saw a bird flying towards me from across the slough, about a mile. It was flying about ten feet above the water, but it didn't fly like a duck or a hawk. As it got closer, I saw it was a young hen pheasant. Reaching the shore, it landed and just sat there, exhausted. Pheasants don't like to fly long distances, and a mile was a long flight for the young bird. After about fifteen minutes, it ran off into the brush.

When I graduated from high school in the spring of 1951, I immediately left for Duluth and Lake Superior to work on the ore boats to make money for college. Because the ore boats don't tie up for the season until late November, I missed the hunting season, but, because the muskrat trapping season started on December 1st, I was able to get busy with that.

I went on the ore boats again in the spring of 1952 and left the boats in late August to begin school at the University of Minnesota in the Agricultural department. Working part time during the week and on some weekends, I still didn't get in much hunting that fall. But on a visit to Wayne in Robbinsdale one weekend, I had another chance to hunt. Wayne's dad, Chester, had a fair hunting dog named Duke, and some hunters wanted Chester and Duke to go hunting with them. Wayne and I would have liked to go along too, but they didn't have room.

Wayne and I felt left out and decided to walk west of Robbinsdale to hunt pheasants. We only had a .22 rifle and a single-shot .410. As I was older, I got the .410.

There had been some snow, but with the warmer weather, only a few patches remained. There were few areas to hunt, and we saw no other hunters, though we heard the occasional shot.

Walking down a gravel road, there was a lone hunter and his dog working a large slough but he was walking across it and didn't work one long narrow portion of it. To me, this was the only area that looked productive to us, so we walked down it, driving the area, side by side with a gap between us. Where there was snow, we looked for pheasant tracks.

After crossing the path of the hunter and dog, I saw a single pheasant track. Following it a short distance, a rooster flew up, and I dropped it.

We went back to the road and headed for home with our one rooster. We had several cars of hunters stop and ask us where we had taken the bird and if we had seen any other pheasants.

Later, when Chester and his party got home, we discovered we had gotten the only bird of the day. They had been skunked.

One Dog, Two Kids

I WAS AT WAYNE'S THE NEXT WEEKEND, and Chester's friends again wanted to hunt pheasants, but, this time, Chester wasn't able to go, so they asked if they could use Chester's Duke. He was reluctant, so they asked if they could use the dog if Wayne and I went with them, too. We were excited, and Chester agreed. I got to use Chester's gun, and I'm not sure where Wayne got his, but he had a shotgun, too.

We drove about 100 miles to hunt near the town of Wood Lake. With the corn picked, we hunted sloughs, fence lines and wood lots as well as stubble fields. Wayne and I were always sent to do the heavy walking, as the hunters usually walked the edges of any rough ground. This worked well for us as we got most of the action, and we discovered why they had such poor luck the previous weekend. Where they wanted to walk, the birds didn't hide.

They were walking about thirty feet apart in a grass slough with a few popple trees when a rooster got up between them. It flew vertically to get out of the sparse trees, then leveled off and flew to new cover.

Wayne and I didn't shoot as we didn't think they could miss the bird, but it was still flying after six shots. This also didn't help their bird count and was typical of their abilities.

Wayne and I also got a pheasant walking a fence line that they had ignored as too thin.

Dang kids!

At the end of the day, I had shot four birds, Wayne had two, and we had doubled up on one, both hitting it. They had one bird amonst them.

It was a rather quiet ride home. When we got home, they asked how we should divide the birds. Because they had taken us, we decided it should be two apiece.

The next year my parents bought the farm near Paynesville, fifty miles to the northeast of the sloughs. Though it offered little hunting opportunities, Herman still had three brothers with farms where we could hunt. Those farms had a nice combination of cornfields and sloughs. I changed my style of hunting on those farms.

Hunting alone, or with only one other hunter, it was difficult to hunt cornfields, but now, with lots of other relatives joining in, hunting the cornfields was possible. We usually had six or seven hunters. Having grown up as a loner, I appreciated the companionship.

It was interesting to post two hunters at the end of the cornfield and have five drivers walk the field to flush the pheasants. Hunting unpicked corn, the drivers would yell out, "Rooster coming your way!" when they saw a bird hoof it down a row. Not being the most willing fliers, pheasants tended to know their terrain and run rather than fly if

97

they felt they had enough cover. Standing corn was plenty of cover for them to hold to the ground.

As only roosters were legal to shoot, when a bird did explode up, if it was a hen, someone was sure to yell, "Hen!" to keep others from reacting to the racket of the bird's take off.

In standing corn, most birds would be running down the rows and many of them the drivers never saw as they moved well in advance of the hunters. But, at the end of the field, they had a problem. That's when they had to find a way to sneak off into a fence row or fly. But that's also where the posted hunters waited, ready.

Oops

ONE OF THE CORN FIELDS WE WORKED had two small grass sloughs. In the first one, we found a newborn calf. We left it, planning to get it back to the barn after we had walked the field. At the second slough, however, we found another newborn calf. The cow had had twins and managed to drop one in each of the sloughs then head back to the barn without either of them. If we hadn't been hunting pheasants that morning, Uncle Louie would have gone out to find the cow's calf, probably reached the one and, since cows didn't have twins very often, not bothered to look for another. That wouldn't have been good for calf number two.

In the mid-1950s, the government began assisting farmers to drain their sloughs to increase crop production. They would pay a large share of the cost of ditching. This practice led to a decline in the pheasant population, not to mention ducks and geese. It also marked a decline in the amount of hunting I did.

Closer to Paradise

In 1962, my wife, daughter of one year, and I moved to St. Cloud, sixty miles northwest of Minneapolis. There I met Ron and again began to enjoy hunting pheasants.

He had some farm relatives in southern Minnesota and had permission to hunt their land. On our first trip, we were a company of three adults, a younger man, and two children, but we all had shotguns.

After hunting the relatives' farm, we got permission to hunt some other area farms. We had good luck and, despite being over 100 miles from home, we decided to come back the next day. Only the young man said he wouldn't be with us the next day.

Being in no hurry, having a whole farm to hunt, we got to the farm well after the 9:00 a.m. opening for the day.

As we drove up, we encountered six hunters who had just finished hunting the farm and were about to leave. Among them was the young man. We weren't particularly happy.

Bad Guess

The next year, we did more scouting and noticed a beautiful slough teaming with ducks, and it didn't appear the slough had often been hunted. With duck season already open, I wondered why this slough hadn't been hunted. I expressed my concerns, but the eldest member of the group said we should hunt it anyway.

On the north side of the slough were a few collapsed buildings from a deserted farmstead. We drove in on the overgrown driveway. One younger hunter and I went to the right, toward a small knoll where we could overlook the slough and watch the other four hunters sneak around the far side.

Waiting for them to fire the first shots, a large flock of ducks flew towards us, and other ducks circled the slough, showing little concern for the hunters. It didn't seem natural to me.

The large flock could see us but continued to fly towards us and would cross directly over us. I didn't shoot. Something just wasn't right, but the younger hunter did and dropped three birds. I yelled to him to quit shooting and head for the cars.

He was confused, of course, so I explained. These ducks had never been hunted here. That made me sure we were hunting illegally. We each hopped into a car and I told him to follow me. We drove about a mile, then stopped. Waiting about half an hour, we drove back to the farm and our irrate buddies. I told them of my concerns. They listened. I suggested we hide the now seven ducks taken by the group and leave the farmyard. We did.

We continued to hunt pheasant in the area that day and came back near sundown to retrieve our ducks. As we were about to leave, an older green pickup with a red, but unlit, light on top of the cab pulled in. An older man stepped out wearing hip boots, and I thought, *Uh-oh, we're in trouble now*.

Our elder stepped out and began some small talk, trying to divert attention from our hunting activities. When the hip-booted man was asked what he was doing on this piece of ground, he said he was trapping muskrats.

The man said, "This is the Fox Lake Game Refuge, and, though trapping is allowed, no duck hunting is." He did say pheasant hunting was also allowed on the farmland as well as trapping.

We thanked the man, a DNR officer, as it turned out, who was trapping on the weekend, and quickly left. A short distance down the road we saw the sign we had missed earlier: "Fox Lake Game Refuge."

Hunting 1, Smell 0

Ron had an elderly friend who raised vizsla dogs. He loved to hunt but was very laid back about it. It became irritating to the rest of us when, whenever we met another hunter, he would have to talk about his dogs, seemingly unaware that the rest of us wanted to be hunting.

Once we went hunting in his van, though we usually preferred to follow in our own car. He always had one or more dogs in his van, and even with the windows open, the smell of dog was pretty overpowering, mostly I think because the dogs spent a lot of time in his van. Ron usually drove alone for obvious reasons.

One Sunday morning, after hunting ducks alone, he went into a cafe for breakfast, still dressed in his camo hunting clothes. Picking up a Sunday paper at the counter, he settled down in a booth with his usual carefree manner to eat and read the paper. It took about twenty minutes before the manager noticed him and came over to apologize for the long wait in taking his order. He said no one had noticed him sitting there waiting. When asked what he had been doing earlier, he said he'd been duck hunting. The manager asked if the camouflage clothing helped.

He said in a sober voice. "It must. I've been sitting here for twenty minutes and nobody saw me."

First Pheasant

As our son Lowell was growing up, I enjoyed exposing him to the outdoors. He had gotten his first duck, so I thought it time to allow him to try for his first pheasant.

Herman's brothers had sold their farms by that time, but we found new and better hunting farther south. We drove to south-central Minnesota and went around to farms, asking for permission to hunt land that seemed promising, but we had little luck.

There was a large county drainage ditch that looked inviting. It varied from six to ten feet deep, with shoulders that were a maze of weeds and brush. With no dog, it would be difficult, but I knew it would hold pheasants.

Hunting one on each side, we struggled up and down the shoulders. After half a mile, Lowell had only seen one hen. When we got back to the car, Lowell was tired, so I decided to walk the ditch on the opposite side of the road. The ditch continued to the west about a quarter of a mile, and then turned to the right to a small hill. A picked cornfield bordered the ditch. After only a few hundred feet, I saw a pheasant leave the cornfield and go into the ditch near the hill. The bird was over 500 feet away, but by the long tail, I could tell it was a rooster.

I went back for Lowell. I told him to walk through the cornfield towards the hill, then walk down to the ditch and choose a spot where he could see over the ditch and the tall grass. When I could see he was ready, I walked quickly to about 100 from where I had seen the pheasant, then slowly walked back and forth on the ditch bank. I was sure this would flush the rooster, but, by the time I made it to Lowell, nothing had flushed.

I then directed Lowell to go out into the cornfield, skirt around the hill and walk down the bank to a good spot. I gave him a few minutes to get set, then began my approach to the hill. I was nearly at the top of the hill when a pheasant flushed and flew directly down the ditch toward Lowell.

It was an easy shot, but, shooting twice, I missed. A second rooster flushed and flew the same route, this time toward Lowell. I swung on that bird and dropped it. I couldn't see Lowell, but I yelled, "Mark the bird!" and started over the hill.

When I came to the other side of the hill and could see Lowell, he was looking across the ditch. I said, "But it fell behind you, back toward the cornfield." He said, "No. It's lying there, across the ditch."

Questioning him again, he said he had heard something fall behind him, but he hadn't looked for that. Searching, I found the pheasant I had dropped about twenty feet behind him.

But he was still looking across the ditch and insisting that there was a pheasant over there, too. Taking off his shoes, he waded across the creek in the bottom of the ditch, climbed the opposite bank and picked up a second rooster.

He had seen the first pheasant and heard me shoot twice as he took aim. We both shot at the same time, neither hearing the other's shot, but we were shooting at different birds.

Congratulating him on his first pheasant, he said he thought I had actually shot it. I could see he wasn't as thrilled as he should have been, so I set out to prove he had killed the bird.

I plucked the feathers off the right side of his bird, showing that it was shot from the right side. Plucking the feathers from my bird, I could show him it had been shot from the rear.

I wanted him to have his first pheasant mounted, as I had done with his first duck, but managed to botch that. A friend said his brother mounted birds and could do it cheaper than the professional taxidermy places. I gave him the job, but the results were horrible. I found out that, in mounting animals as in many things in life, you get what you pay for. I have since heard of many instances of prized birds and animals discarded because of poor workmanship in mounting. This included a black bear take out and a bobcat some friends had.

My Last Pheasant?

WITH WORKING AND RAISING A FAMILY and the decline in the pheasant and duck populations, my hunting time turned from birds to deer. My most recent pheasant hunt, and possibly my last, came in 2006 at the age of seventy-three after not having shot at a pheasant in sixteen years. I had been hunting deer on my brother-in-law's farm, but I had seen and heard several pheasants.

On Friday evening, a week after deer season, we had a light, fluffy snow that continued into Saturday morning. I thought this would give me a really perfect opportunity to track pheasants.

When deer hunting, I had been in the woods on the north side of a cornfield, which also had woods on its south side. A narrow field road on the south side, between the cornfield and woods provided access. Jutting out into the cornfield from the access road was a small grass slough with brush at its northeast corner.

Saturday morning was beautiful, with temperatures in the twenties and a very light snow still falling. Maybe an inch had fallen overnight over an existing six inches.

I had not used my shotgun in years, but I had put optic sights on it when I put them on my first deer rifle, the famous Winchester Model 94.

Walking down the trail, the only track was from a squirrel searching out a forgotten ear of corn. I made my way to the slough, but there were no pheasant trails. Walking through the slough, suddenly I heard the raucus cackle of a rooster as it flushed from the brush. It was winging for safety in the woods to the north.

I think I was expecting to shoot like in my youth, when I could wisk the gun to my shoulder, point, shoot, and seldom miss. Time changes things. My first shot was a clean miss, and I told myself, *Aim!*

At the second shot, the bird shuddered, attempted to stay flying, but after seventy-five feet glided into the corn stubble well short of the woods. It had been an extremely long shot, but I had #4 shot.

Expecting the bird to run and hide, I decided to walk a box around it and look for tracks as it tried to escape on the ground. Going far to the east, I then walked to the north beyond where the bird had landed, then to the west. I saw no tracks.

Walking back, I found the pheasant lying against a cornstalk, pretty much where it had landed. Lifting it, I could still feel a little pulse, but I didn't want to wring the neck on this beautiful bird. Instead I carried it back to the trail and laid it in some weeds.

I continued hunting for about two hours, seeing many fresh tracks and a few pheasants, but only a hen came within range. Coming back to the slough through the woods to the south, as I stepped onto the trail, a second pheasant flew up, again heading to the north.

I again missed on my first shot and, after telling myself to aim, at the second shot it dropped. Just like the first bird, except that this had been an even longer shot than the first. The bird fluttered the same as the first pheasant and, after about fifty feet, glided into the corn stubble.

Again walking my box route, I found no tracks and again finally discovered the bird lying where it had landed only about thirty feet from where the first pheasant had landed.

Though I hadn't had the skill of my youth, I was excited about shooting at the only two roosters I had seen and, after sixteen years, had dropped them both.

With the second rooster in hand, I went back to retrieve the first pheasant, but it wasn't where I had left it. I found the small depression in the snow it had made when I laid it down, but no bird. Thinking it might have been a dog or fox that stole my prize, I was surprised not to find any tracks. *Perhaps it was an eagle*, I thought. But a bird of prey would have left the imprint of its wings or feet in the new snow. Yet the only marks in the snow were from the pheasant. My pheasant had recovered, and I had shot it twice.

I left the pheasant for my brother-in-law, but later I wished I had checked where the BBs had hit.

13

Grouse

IN MY YOUTH I KNEW OF NO GROUSE in Central Minnesota and wasn't aware of them until the early 1950s when I was fishing in northern Minnesota. Near the fishing lake, there were miles of logging roads

going off into the woods, and those dirt roads offered great grouse hunting. Walking just a few miles of them, I could be assured of a limit of four.

When our son was four, and our daughter seven, we camped in the woods for the weekend during grouse season. Since this was 1969, and the height of the grouse population had been in the 1950s, birds were harder to find. Lowell and I walked the trail for about two hours, with no luck. On the way back to camp, he was tired, so I put him on my shoulders.

As we neared an excavation, where soil had been removed along the trail, a grouse flew up from within the excavation. I yelled for Lowell to "Hang on!" and raised my gun. As the grouse rose to the top of the excavation and turned into the woods, I shot, and it dropped.

Getting back to the camper, my wife said she had seen a cat walk by on the trail. I was surprised, as we were miles from any house. I asked if it had a tail, and she hesitated for a few seconds, then said, "Well, a really short one." She had seen a young bobcat, a rare and fortuitous sighting.

Crude hunting shelter.

Camping in the Rough

As Lowell grew older, but not old enough to hunt, I would take him with me when I went up in late October to check my deer stands. My stands were near my favorite location, the "Beaver Pond," about a mile back into the woods. It was a deeper pond than many in the area and about 300 feet across, surrounded by popple, birch, and tall white pines.

On the northwest corner was a small creek leading to two other shallow sloughs extending about half a mile to the north. The pond held one beaver lodge that had steadily been enlarged over the years. On the southwest corner was the end of one of the old logging trails, which left a small level area in the woods. A large tree had fallen across the area, and that was always our picnic table, where we would meet for drives on the deer hunts.

We would leave the car with only my shotgun, shells, a knife, salt, pepper, matches and a double sleeping bag. Our supplies were stashed off along the trail as we walked the trails, hunting grouse until about 3:00, and then pick up our supplies and head back to the beaver pond for the night.

We would find an open area in the woods to place our sleeping bags, clearing the area of any accumulated sticks and branches and stones. Fallen branches became our small camp fire, and an A-frame shelter held our gear. Being long past a killing frost, we had little vegetation to cover the A-frame, and usually just left the open branches for cover. It was beautiful to look up through the branches at the stars and moon on a clear night.

After collecting wood and building our campfire, we next addressed our supper. That meant we needed to clean and dress the gouse and build a framework with green branches to sit above the fire to roast the grouse. As we had brought for supplies only salt and pepper, out meal consisted of fire-roasted grouse seasoned with our salt and pepper. It might have been a simple meal, but, after a day in the woods, it was amazingly delicious.

A small creek supplied our drinking water and a place to wash up before and after our meal.

Then, we would sit around the fire until about 10:00, enjoying the evening before crawling into our sleeping bags. I always found it interesting to listen to the sounds of the woods at night.

One night Lowell felt something pulling his hair. Waking and turning quickly, he saw a mouse run into the leaves. Another time, having gone to bed under a brilliant night sky with stars and moon, I woke up at 1:00 to snow flakes. With only the branches of trees for shelter, the snow was falling straight through onto our sleeping bags. Lowell had his head tucked into his sleeping bag and wasn't even aware that it had begun to snow. But, even with the snow, we had to stay where we were because it would have been too difficult to find our way back to our car without flashlights, and we always traveled with the bare minimum of equipment.

I lay awake and, every few minutes, kicked at the sleeping bag to dislodge the snow. After about an hour and a half, the snow stopped with about an inch of accumulation.

The Next Morning

When Lowell was about fourteen, he and his friend Pat and I decided to camp out in the middle of January. We planned it several months in advance, knowing extreme cold or heavy snow could cancel our plans . . . or make it a great adventure. We were looking for a true wilderness experience with the winter weather as one of the challenges we would face.

As the trip was planned well past any hunting season, we planned to take hot dogs and snack food and use snow for our water. We would have to wear warm clothes, bring cold-rated sleeping bags and build an A-frame shelter in the woods.

We planned to camp on the north side of the beaver pond, under some tall pines, where we could get some boughs for our stick-frame shelter and to lay on the frozen, snow-covered ground to give us some insulation between it and our sleeping bags.

The weather was somewhat of a disappointment as it was only twelve degrees at night, and there was actually some thawing going on during the day, which turned the snow a little soft and slushy.

We got our shelter set up, however, and collected a supply of wood for our campfires, having to trudge through over a foot of snow to do it. Had it been colder, we would have been able to walk on top of most of the snow.

We expected to see some wildlife, but hadn't realized how quiet the woods was in the dead of winter. Our activity had alerted everything in the area that we were there. Little was moving. I had brought along a couple weasel traps, but we only found two sets of tracks. We saw no deer trails, and few other tracks. Our plan was to check our traps in the morning, then head home.

We enjoyed our supper by the fire, but there was such an eerie silence that it began to creep us out. We heard none of the night sounds we had heard in the fall.

The fire gave us some heat, but we had expected a greater challenge with colder weather. We had wanted more for a January camp out.

In the morning, we checked the traps and had caught one weasel. We packed up, cleaned up our camp site and left with little interest in a second trip. But the trip gave us a greater appreciation of nature and what the resident birds and animals had to endure in the winter.

Part Three

Deer Hunting

14

My First Deer Hunt

My first deer hunt was a disappointment, but also humorus, looking at my lack of knowledge. Deer frequented our farm but were seldom seen. By the age of fifteen, I had only seen eight or nine. When I saw a deer, it was an occurrence worthy of telling friends and neighbors. Because we had no large woods on our land, on my first hunt, I decided to sit in our pasture near a small creek where I had seen deer tracks. Not realizing a hunter should use camouflage, I just sat there in jeans and sweatshirt with my shotgun loaded with slugs across my lap. I did see two deer but long after they had seen me.

The next year a neighbor, Bill Weise, felt sorry for me and invited me to hunt deer with his group in northern Minnesota. They all had rifles, and I had my shotgun.

Going to their deer stands early in the morning, Bill put me in a stand nearest the farm. It was up in a pine tree on what they called "gut run." In previous years, a hunter had gotten three deer in one day from that stand. Bill pointed to the northeast and said, "When the sun comes up, you'll see a large pine tree. It's near the farm. If you want to leave the woods early, go towards that pine tree." He and a friend headed to the northwest through the woods. I thought the dry leaves sounded so noisy and loud. I thought this was great. I should hear anything coming near my tree.

About twenty minutes later, just as it was getting light enough to see, I heard the crunching of leaves. Something was coming my way from the southwest. As the sound grew louder, I recognized Bill and his friends just about the same time they saw me. They had gotten confused on their way to their stand. They had intended to be heading northwest, but somehow had managed to circle back to where I was. It indicated to me just how easy it was to get lost. Embarrassed, they struck out again for the other stand, not saying a word.

Of the five of us, none saw a deer, and at noon, Bill decided to make a drive though a small section of meadow and brush. He told another hunter and me to post on the far end, as the three others waited to make the drive.

We had just gotten set where we were supposed to post when we heard two shots and then some loud talking. They called us back to them. We found them standing over a strange-looking buck deer. It was a mule deer, the first Bill had heard about in this area. Some were known to be on the western border of the state, but to his knowledge, never in north central Minnesota.

It was a beautiful deer, with a large rack, a distinctive black stripe down the back and a tail different from the whitetail that inhabited most of the state.

This was on the first day of the season, but there was a flesh wound on one of the deer's flanks, a graze from a rifle. But it had started to heal, so it couldn't have happened that morning. Bill's friend's wife cleared up this mystery. She said she had taken a shot at a deer a few days earlier. She said it had been a strange-looking deer. She thought she had missed.

Nobody Told Me!

In the fall of 1950, my cousin Wayne came out to hunt deer at the farm. We decided to hunt in the woods to the east of the slough as I had seen no signs of deer elsewhere. I picked a stand on the northeast corner of a large slough, and he went north into the woods.

I was along the bottom edge of the slough, with some woods to my northwest, a hill to the north and east covered with tall grass and brush, and over the hill to the east a fence and pasture.

At mid-morning, a large buck jumped the fence, coming from the pasture and stood broadside to me at about about forty yards. I had never seen a deer this big or this close. I raised by gun and pulled the trigger, but nothing happened. I lowered the gun to check the safety, and it was off. I raised the gun again, aimed, and the same thing happened. Nothing. The deer was intently watching something to the east, back in the pasture, and hadn't noticed my movements.

Confused by what was happening, I dropped the gun to my waist to check it, and, in doing so, the pump clicked. It hadn't been pushed far enough ahead. But, at the click, the deer turned toward the pasture. I raised the gun again and fired, but the deer was already moving and cleared the fence. In a moment, it had disappeared.

I was disappointed at how I could miss a deer when I seldom missed a bird. I quickly got over it, though, as I had already become accustomed to disappointment in deer hunting.

Hearing my shot, Wayne rushed back, and I told him my story. As it was near noon by now, we decided to go back to the farm for dinner and come back out later in the afternoon.

Getting back about 3:00, I put Wayne where I had been, and I went further back into the woods. It was very quiet. And we heard no shots.

As dusk was setting in, I heard Wayne shoot, and I rushed back to see if he had gotten a deer. He said a buck had jumped the fence, coming from the pasture to the east, and then continued west towards the woods. He had gotten off a shot. He said the deer had stumbled, and it looked like he had injured it.

I followed Wayne as we walked into the woods where the deer had disappeared. We had gone only about fifty yards when we found his buck. Wayne was younger than I was, and this was his first deer hunt. We soon realized that the deer was too heavy to drag home, and I hadn't thought to bring a knife to gut it. Nobody had told me that was how it was done. I didn't usually gut my birds in the field, after all.

We decided to go back to the farm for a kitchen knife. As we were about to leave, two other hunters appeared, having heard our shot as they were about to leave the woods. They looked at our deer, and I mentioned that we didn't have a knife with us. They offered me theirs. They said they had just gutted a buck deer in the pasture, less than 100 yards east of the fence where mine had disappeared that morning. They had been hunting northeast of us and had seen no deer, but when they were walking back to their car, they found this dead, freshly shot deer.

The hunter said he owned Bergquist Signs in Willmar, and I could bring the knife to his office.

Wayne and I enjoyed dragging the deer the three-quarters of a mile to the farm. We were lucky it was a buck so we could hang onto the rack as a good handle to drag it by as we had no rope either. Nobody had told me to bring a rope along on a deer hunt.

I brought the knife back to Bergquist Signs the next day, and Mr. Bergquist asked if I would like to work for him in his sign business. I was in my senior year of high school but he said I could work part time until school let out, then go to full time.

I enjoyed working for Mr. Bergquist but I had plans to go to agricultural school at the University of Minnesota in the fall. I had had a bad case of asthma when I was ten to fourteen, but it had improved. Having no other training, I thought I'd try agriculture. The tuition was only twenty dollars a month, and I worked part time to support myself, as my parents weren't able to help financially.

I was able to get home for deer hunting, though, and anxious to get back into the woods. My parents had moved to the new farm thirty miles to the northeast by this time, near Paynesville, and, having no other place to hunt, I went back to the sloughs for hopes of my first deer.

Wayne's deer.

15

Lucky Fox

It was cold, with over a foot of snow on the level, and many two- to four-foot drifts. I went back to where I had hunted earlier. The snow made for difficult walking, but I had great visibility and would be able to track deer easily. I saw no tracks of other hunters. I assumed they would be coming from the north being much closer to the road there.

The fresh snow defined the edge of the slough, and it was beautiful, and I noticed a narrow grass slough angling back to the east along the south side of the pasture. I was enjoying the beauty of the area when I heard an eerie scream from south of the pasture. This was followed by several more screams of panic, and then silence. I wasn't sure, but those screams sounded like they could have been human. That made me nervous.

A short time later, a red fox appeared from the south, walking north through the slough, heading for the woods. It would be walking my me at about sixty yards at the most, barely within shotgun range with the early type slugs. The screams I had heard earlier apparently came when the fox had caught a rabbit. It had either eaten that rabbit or stashed it for a future meal, and was now heading for a safe place to rest.

This was the first live fox I had seen, and it was beautiful, its red coat against the fresh snow even more brilliant than I could imagine. The black accents on its face the perfect highlights. As it plodded through the deep snow, its nose pointed ahead, alert for danger, with his carefully fluffed tail just skimming the top of the snow.

I was impressed by the animal's beauty, but having heard the pride of those hunters able to bag a fox, I also saw this moment as an opportunity. In the back of my mind, I also was calculating the value of the fur. I raised my shotgun, aimed and fired. The fox stumbled, and I could see it was hit in the upper right leg as it ran towards the woods. I immediately took up the chase, tracking it into the woods, passing another deer hunter. The fox ran past his stand, but he didn't shoot. He said the right shoulder was injured.

Proceeding a short distance beyond the hunter, I heard some crashing in the brush and looked up to see a deer rushing right towards me. It saw me just as I saw it, and it made a sharp turn into some thick brush at about forty yards. I got off a quick shot. I heard a few seconds of noise in the brush, and then silence. Following the deer's trail in the snow, I came upon it again. I was about thirty yards away when it jumped up from the snow, attempting to hightail it deeper into the brush. I got off a second shot. The doe had been hit the first time about four inches in front of the tail, a wound just scraping the back bone. It was a serious wound but not one to drop the deer immediately or keep it down. My second shot finished the job.

This time, I had brought a knife to gut the deer, but still had managed to forget a rope. It was a tough drag (no antlers to hold onto this time) over and through the snow drifts, dragging it by the head the half mile to the road. Still, I was very excited. As I neared the road, a school friend, Manly, who had also been hunting, drove by and stopped to help me drag the deer through the ditch and into my car trunk. I was sweaty and exhausted, but thrilled.

Reliving

I HAD RELIVED MY EXPERIENCE at the bunk many times, but it wasn't until I shot at my second deer that I realized what had really happened.

Hunting ducks and pheasants, I was used to shooting and having my target drop. I really thought that would be the case with deer. Mr. Bergquist had retrieved my deer, not having known who had shot it. I think he could have given it to me if he knew. I realized it was likely they had driven the deer to Wayne, so we had benefited each other.

I learned quickly one shot didn't always drop a deer. Wounded animals had to be tracked. I learned to look for blood as well as tracks.

After the year of Agriculture School, I realized I wouldn't be able to farm because of my asthma, and I decided to go to Dunwoody, a trade school, but I needed to earn some money first.

I had a cousin who worked on the ore boats out of Duluth. He said I would enjoy the work, and I could save some money. I worked a full season, well into December, and then left the boats in August of the second year to start school. With school, and then a job, I wasn't able to hunt deer again until 1957.

Great Friends

HAVING FISHED AN ISOLATED LAKE near Park Rapids in Northern Minnesota, I became friends with Jim Dank and his sons: Bob, Clayton, and Larry. They lived in the woods near the lake with a frugal lifestyle, but they were very content. Hunting deer, grouse, and ducks, along with fishing supplied most of their meat supply. I ate many meals of canned venison they had put up during deer season. They planted a large garden each year as well. Jim had a small dozer and did some excavation and landscaping jobs.

I was amazed that, having so little, they could be so considerate of others. Knowing I enjoyed deer hunting, they invited me to hunt with them on opening day in 1957.

Getting to their house well before dawn, I expected them to be ready to go. I was taught that one should be in the woods and set well before dawn. But, having the entire season to hunt, they were in no rush. This was their greatest excitement of the year, and they would hunt the full season. It was well after sunrise, therefore, before we left for the hunting location west of Lake George. There we were joined by the rest of our hunting party, which now numbered thirteen.

It was about an hour and a half after sunrise before we entered the woods, and they knew these woods well. Clayton was a couple of years younger than I was, but he was to be my guide. We were about a quarter mile into the woods, when we met a young hunter going back to the road. Clayton stopped to talk with him, but I was anxious to continue to our stands. As they were talking, I was observing the woods and saw a deer running through the woods about eighty yards away, and, oddly, always running to our left. I called to the other two, and they jumped into action, but they also ended up blocking my view as they shot. I then picked an area to the east where it might be possible to see a deer run through, and aimed down the opening. Having a shotgun, not a rifle, I would have less range and would have to aim high so that the heavy slug found its target.

A few seconds after they shot, I saw the blur of deer entering the small open space I was covering. I had been aiming higher and had to lower my sight and shoot in a split second without taking careful aim.

Clayton and the other hunter went to check out where they had shot at their deer, and I went to where I had shot at mine. I found an explosion of blood in the grass and brush and a heavy blood trail. Following the blood trail for only a few yards, I found a dead spike buck.

Clayton had found some hair where a shot may have grazed a deer, but there was no blood. He said he was sure he had missed. The young hunter said nothing.

Hearing my yell, they came over to my deer. My shot had shattered its heart. Clayton congratulated me, but the young hunter still remained silent.

121

Dragging the deer back to the trail, we passed another hunter who had been deer hunting near us. The deer may ahve been as close to him as to me when I shot. Without being asked, he said, "The third shot hit the deer." He said he had heard the thump of the bullet. I asked Clayton how many shots they had taken, and he said one each. Getting to the road, we went right to join our part, and the other hunter turned left.

Waiting by the cars, two of our group soon returned from the trail we had walked. They had met the young hunter who told them someone had stolen his deer. Mine was the only deer shot by our group that day.

The next weekend, I was again invited to hunt with Jim and his boys, but at a new location west of Lake George. This time it was just Jim, Clayton, the two younger boys, Bob, Larry, and me.

The area was wild, but it was well known by Jim and Clayton, as they had hunted it for years. There was a north-south creek meandering along the west side of our hunting area, and Jim said if I got lost to head west to the creek and follow it downstream to the road. It was an easy area to get lost in, as I soon found out.

I am not sure if the younger boys were old enought to hunt, but they were told to stay near the cars. A large fire was built to keep them warm. Jim and Clayton went to the north and northeast and suggested I didn't need to go far from the cars. We were to gather back at the cars at noon. We saw no deer but had heard a couple of shots to our north.

After the shots, Clayton heard someone yell and later another yell. He heard more yelling after that but from different locations, but the tone began to sound frantic.

It had quieted down by noon, but Jim thought he and Clayton should go into the area to see if someone was injured, lost or in some kind of trouble.

Scary

In mid afternoon, the boys were startled by the sound of something bursting through the brush, something noisier than a deer. As they were standing by the fire, warming up, a hunter approached from the north, apparently attracted by the flames of the fire glinting through the trees. He was rushing through the brush, dragging his rifle by the barrel with his clothes torn by the brush. The boys were scared.

As he got closer to the fire, he stopped, staring at the boys a few seconds, and possibly realizing it wasn't members of his own party, he took off to the east , still dragging his rifle.

Near sunset, they heard some more noise in the brush approaching from the northeast. It was the same hunter, this time minus his rifle and cap, and with bloody scratches on his face and hands. He again stopped, stared and left.

In the late afternoon, I had heard six or seven shots to the north that appeared to be of a pistol, not a rifle. Coming back to camp, Clayton was dragging a Canada goose. The goose had been swimming in the creek, and he'd shot it.

During the week, Clayton h ad hunted this area, and he had shot at a flock of high-flying geese, hitting one in the wing. He couldn't find the goose, but, during the week, it had apparently found the creek, and he finished it off with his pistol.

Jim was concerned about the possibly lost hunter. On our way out, we stopped at the Lake George store, told them our story, and asked if anyone had been reported missing. None had. Jim checked during the week, and there still were no reports of lost hunters. We all hoped that meant that the distressed hunter apparently found his own group or they found him. In explaining his bizarre behavior, Jim said he might have been in such panic that he would only seek help from members of his own hunting party. This was typical when in a panic.

16

Bow Hunting

Morning Panic

THE EVENING BEFORE DEER SEASON, I would usually go to my parents' farm in Paynesville, getting up about 12:00 and leaving for hunting at 1:00 in the morning to make the three-and-one-half-hour drive that would include a ritual stop for breakfast. I would usually come back that night, making it a very long day.

I often had some excitement during my drive. One morning, with little traffic, at 2:00 a.m., I was driving maybe ten miles per hour over the speed limit when I noticed car lights rapidly gaining on me. They slowed down to follow me. I then noticed the red bubble on the car. I thought it best not to slow down, but to keep the same speed, making sure I drove a straight line. After about a minute, the car passed and the driver waved as he went by. It was a highway patrol, and probably also a deer hunter.

One morning at 2:00 a.m., coming over a large hill, I saw a car parked on the shoulder of the road, well up ahead, with the blinkers on. There was a car ahead of me, and as we approached the parked car, the car in front of me applied its brakes and made an abrupt stop on the shoulder of the road, alongside a crippled deer, lying on the highway. The first car had hit the deer, and it lay in the center of the road, struggling to get up. It apparently had a broken back. I had no time to stop and had to try to squeeze between the deer and the parked car. I was fortunate the animal was lying to the left of the center line. When I neared it, it struggled to leap into my headlights. As I passed, its head was facing me only inches from my side window.

Visiting my parents on many weekeneds, I became friends with two neighbor boys, Woody and Burt Manz, who were about ten years younger than I was, and they became the brothers I would have liked to have had. I would take them summer and winter fishing, and, as they got older, we all began bow hunting.

These were the days of the stright fiberglass bows, but I was lucky enough to have upgraded to a laminated recurve.

First Bow Hunt

A POPULAR LOCATION TO BOW HUNT was at Camp Ripley, a National Guard training center in Central Minnesota. It had a large acreage and abundant deer. People were allowed to come in during the week to scout for deer, but hunting was only open for two weekends, and only for bow hunting.

Cars of hunters lined up waiting for the gate to open about 4:30 a.m., and then there was bedlam, with hunters trying to be first to their chosen locations.

We had no chosen location, so we just drove into the center of the camp and picked a spot. With that many hunters all over the place, deer would be running every which way.

Burt had the only shot, hitting a doe. We found no blood trail and decided to go back to the car for dinner, let it lie down and search for it later. As we were eating our lunch, with our bows lying on the ground, Woody placed his razor sharp arrow head against a bow string, and asked Burt to dare him to cut it. Burt looked down at the bow, and dared him.

The bow flew back as the string was cut, and Burt said, check the bow. The bows were nearly identical, and Woody had just cut his own string. We had to drive to town for a new bow string. This was typical for the boys, always enjoyable to be with.

Their mother had a treadle sewing machine, and one of the boys put his fingers beneath the needle and dared the other to pump the foot pedal. As the needle went through his finger, the first brother jerked back breaking off the needle. There weren't many dares they wouldn't accept. That made me realize how much I had missed by not having a brother.

Going back to search for Burt's deer, we had no luck, but another hunter had seen the arrow in the deer, and someone else may have harvested it.

Stolen Deer

THE NEXT YEAR, THEIR DAD, HAROLD, decided to go with us to bow hunt at Camp Ripley in the morning, and then we would go to Park Rapids to hunt grouse in the afternoon. That year I had scouted Camp Ripley and found a beautiful deer crossing at Cody Road and another road. There was an east-west trail and a crossing trail northwest to southeast. Standing to the northeast twenty yards off the trails, I had a beautiful location. Harold and the boys went to the northwest to hunt.

We had gotten to our locations early, and I had been in my stand only a few minutes when I saw another hunter walking towards me from the east. He apparently had the same plan as I had and had picked out the same location. He saw me and walked back up the trail, taking a stand about eighty yards away, across the swale to the east.

About 9:00, I heard a deer approaching from the northeast, coming up the swale, but still out of sight. As it was about to clear the top of the ridge, about twenty-five yards from me, the hunter to the east shot. That shot had to be about sixty to seventy yards and well out of range, and, of course, he missed. I believe his intent was to scare the deer to eliminate my chances of a good shot.

A short time later, he came over to talk, but I was only interested in hunting. He was much older than I was, and I didn't want to be disrespectful, so I listened. As he talked, I kept watching the trails, when a huge buck came bounding towards us down the trail to the west, I pointed and whispered, "Deer." With the deer still fifty yards away, the old guy quickly raised his bow, and I followed suit.

Seeing us at about thirty yards, the buck veered to the right into the woods. We both shot, and we saw one arrow embed in the deer's flank. He said, "I hit it!"

He was shooting white arrows, and I had orange. I thought the arrow in the deer had been one of my orange ones, but I didn't say anything. We both started walking towards where the deer had been hit, and we found his white arrow embedded in a popple tree. There was a heavy blood trail, and after about fifty yards, we found my arrow. It was intact, with blood about five inches up the shaft. It had apparently been pulled out by the deer. The hunter said, "You have yourself a deer. You cut an artery for sure. It'll quickly bleed out." He suggested I not trail the deer right away but give it time to lie down and bleed out.

I yelled to Harold and the boys, and they quickly came back to see what had happened. I was excited and glad Harold was there. He had more experience. He suggested we wait another half hour. He then suggested I follow the blood trail while they would fan out on either side.

Walking only about 150 yards, I found a large mass of blood on the leaves where the buck had apparently lain down on its wound.

As Harold and the boys came over, five hunters from the town of Bovey rushed over and said, "Someone has your deer." They had seen the deer lay down and tried to surround it when it jumped up. It ran up a hill towards another hunter standing by a tree.

As it ran, its tongue was hanging out and its left hind quarter was a mass of blood and foam. It ran toward the hunder and dropped about twenty feet away, practically landing at his feet, without his having to take a shot. Two young hunters then quickly backed up in a yellow Chevy station wagon, loaded up the deer and took off.

As it was near noon, we decided to leave to hunt grouse. Leaving the camp, we stopped at the gate where they checked and weighed each deer shot in the camp. I wanted to show them my arrow and tell them my story. I was surprised to discover that one of the two DNR people at the gate, Lytle, had been my teacher at college. They said they would watch for a yellow Chevy and check out any deer the hunters had. They also looked at my arrow.

We had good luck on grouse that afternoon, but my mind wasn't on the grouse hunting. I was staying with my cousins near Minneapolis, and getting back Sunday evening, I gave them my story. He had also been at Ripley that day and said he'd heard two deer had been stolen. He said the other deer had fallen and was lying on the ground when a hunter walked up, put an arrow into the deer and claimed it.

At midweek, there was a picture and story in the *Minneapolis Tribune* of the two huge deer from Camp Ripley tied to the finders of a yellow Chevrolet station wagon. The deer were 235 pounds and 238 pounds respectively, and the picture was taken at Corey's Sporting Goods, three blocks from the office where I worked, 1004 Marquette Avenue. I would walk over to Corey's at least once a week, and had become good friends with their archery expert, Bruce, who had taken the picture. Bruce said the one buck had only a single wound in the left hing quarter and was told it was shot at about seven yards. One of the hunters was from a Minneapolis suburb, and the other was from Central Minnesota.

I looked up their addresses and was going to call them, but then I thought it would only cause me more pain.

Going back to Ripley the next weekend, Lytle confirmed my story. In checking the yellow station wagon with two large deer, he said my arrow also fit the single wound in the hind quarter. He said the deer shot in the hind quarter was the one weighing 235 pounds, the fifth largest deer shot in Camp Ripley at that time.

I moved to St. Cloud in 1962, and a few years later was working with a young man with the same last name as one of the hunters who took my deer. I asked if he knew the hunter who had taken it. He said he did. It was his brother. I told him my story and he said, "Yes, he has a large buck on the wall that was shot at Ripley." He mentioned it to his brother, but he denied it. I had been told his partner had taken the two deer and kept the largest for himself.

I never met or talked with the man but was shown his picture, and he apparently knew who I was.

One evening at a PTA meeting, he was sitting two rows ahead of my wife and me and I called to him. "Hi _____."

He turned, stared at me and turned back. A few minutes later, he got up and moved several rows behind me.

His brother was going to get me a picture of the deer, but it was destroyed in a fire before he got the chance.

Looking for the Poacher

In 1958, I bought a Winchester Model 94 .30-.30 rifle for fifty dollars as I planned to hunt in northern Minnesota, out of the shotgun area. I bought the rifle only a month before deer season. A week before the season opening, I had yet to shoot the rifle or check it out. There are laws against firing a rifle in the woods within nine days of deer season, so, the Saturday before deer season, my fiancee and I took a day trip to Duluth, and I threw my new gun in the trunk, thinking I might have a chance to fire it.

It was near sundown, and we were still in Duluth, when I remembered I had to shoot my rifle. We quickly drove south of town, found some narrow, gravel roads, looking for a place to set up a target and sight in the rifle. We finally drove by a small gravel pit, turned around and drove in.

Having only an eight-and-one-half-by-eleven-inch sheet of paper for a target, I put an ink mark in the center and set it up against the gravel bank. Taking two quick shots, I saw they were both within a four-inch circle, and I was satisfied.

We quickly exited the pit and headed back down the gravel roads. We had gotten less than half a mile when we met a slow-moving car with three men in it, all scanning the wood. I assumed they were looking for a poacher.

17

Memorable Hunts

First Big Buck

THAT FALL JIM AGAIN INVITED ME TO HUNT with them, and I now had more range with my .30-.30. We hunted on a large tract of land called "Rusty Hanson's Ranch." It had a large grass meadow with great terrains and woods, and miles of trails, many constructed and maintained by Jim. These were mostly used for grouse hunting. There was a gate by the highway that was closed during the summer, but opened for deer season. The place also had a ranch house and out buildings on the south side of the meadow, and these were used during deer hunting by small groups of hunters. Most hunted south of the ranch house and appreciated the few hunters to the north chasing deer toward them.

We parked on the north side of the meadow, with Jim, Clayton, and Bob hunting a series of trails and ridges to the northwest. Jim knew these woods from over forty years of hunting the Ranch, and he liked to do both walking and still hunting and knew what to expect over the next ridge.

Jim asked if I would take the youngest son, Larry, with me and pick a stand location to the northeast, but he told us not to go too far back into the woods.

Walking about 200 yards down a wooded ridge, I placed Larry where he could look across a swale onto the opposite ridge. I proceeded another 200 yards and posted where I could look into and across a swale.

About 9:30, I noticed a deer coming from the north, walking to the southwest towards Larry, at about 150 yards. It would be a long shot, and with my lack of experience with my new gun and open sights, I decided not to shoot. I expected this would give Larry a shot. About twenty minutes later, the deer came back, going back to the northeast. It had probably seen Larry, and was backtracking.

This time, it was on the opposite ridge, and it would be a long shot for me, but I had to try. Raising the rifle and trying to line up the sights in the open area in the brush where I expected it would walk. As I got ready for the shot, the deer turned and walked down the slope directly towards me. I picked out a spot where it would pass between two trees. When it appeared there, I shot. It dropped, hit in the spine. This was a beautiful, well-matched ten-pointer.

I was always excited to see a deer, but I was never very nervous. I believe that was from being raised on a farm and being used to animals. I always took care on my first shot, knowing it would probably be my best, if not only, chance.

Later in the day, Jim showed me a small lake east of the meadow that was called Camp 4 from the logging days. Near the north end of the lake was a salt lick, also left over from earlier times. In the 1930s, they would throw salt into the sand used to make ice roads safer and also "salt" an area for the deer. In the spring, deer would ingest the sand to get the salt. The area was about twenty feet across, and in some places up to two feet had been eaten away. Salt was important to deer in the spring as they began to feed on fresh greenery and begin to build up their weight and strength after the long, lean winter months.

I would always see many tracks in the spring in that locale, but very few in the fall.

There used to be a law against putting out salt licks as many thought it was meant to attract deer during the hunting season. I believe it is now legal because people have begun to realize that deer use salt licks in the spring to supplement their diets, and not during the fall hunting season.

A "Missed" Season

I became engaged in 1958, and we planned to be married in the fall of 1959. As I was an avid hunter and fisherman, the staff at the office was always asking when I was getting married. I would reply, "Between duck and pheasant seasons," or "Between pheasant and deer seasons." We were planning a reception at the Moose Lodge in St. Cloud, but the only fall weekend available was on the opening of deer season, November 7, 1959. The reason was obvious. I asked my fiancee about hunting on her dad's farm early in the morning, but that got me nowhere. Woody, my best man, with Burt and Harold did get an early-morning hunt in before the festivities.

During the summer, when I had been fishing with the Manzes near Park Rapids, they met Jim, and he also invited them to hunt with him, as it was usually the more the merrier at the "Ranch." Jim, who preferred to walk the woods always got his fair share of the deer, and he always seemed to know where everyone else was and would attempt to drive deer to the other hunters. He seemed to enjoy other hunter's success as much as his own.

I brought Wayne, and with the Manzes, there would be five of us, plus Jim and his boys. Meeting Jim on the north side of the meadow, we again did not enter the woods until after sun up. Jim took Manzes with him to the northwest, and Wayne was going to wait until they got in the woods and then walk a trail to the north.

I went into the woods to the northeast, back about three-quarters of a mile, and stood on a hill on the north side of a slough. Near noon, a doe came bounding over a hill from the west, and then stopped behind some heavy brush on the hillside to my south. I could see only the shadow of the deer. It appeared nervous, looking back toward the west. I couldn't see enough to get off a shot, but after standing for about a minute, it bounded off to the east.

I got off a shot as it was about to enter the woods, but it did not act like it was hit. Walking to where it had been when I shot, I found some blood and what Jim later told me was a fragment of lung. Fifty yards further into the woods, I found the doe. I was just beginning to dress the deer when Jim appeared from the west. Knowing where I would be hunting, he had driven the doe to me. Instead of dragging the deer back through the woods, he suggested I go east to the trail and follow it back to the meadow.

Getting back to the cars about 3:00, I found a group of three killed deer, a buck, a doe, and a fawn lying on the ground, waiting to be loaded up. Near sundown, Manzes came back and the deer were not theirs, as they had seen no deer. A short time later, Wayne came down the trail, all smiles. He had walked the trail only a short way in the morning when a doe and fawn crossed ahead of him. The fawn made the fatal mistake of pausing in the middle of the trail. Wayne harvested it.

He took the time to dress the fawn, then continued down the trail. Going again only a short way, he spotted a doe standing in the woods just off the trail. He again scored. It may have been the mother and was waiting for the fawn. After dressing the doe, he again set off down the trail, but he didn't get far. Approaching the meadow, he scared up a buck across the meadow. It headed up a hill. Wayne got off about six shots, he said, before the deer disappeared over the hill. He began trailing the buck and found it down just over the hill. What a day!

Jim had gotten no deer, but he wasn't concerned. Instead, he suggested we give two of the deer to the Manzes as they had gotten nothing and Jim and his boys had the rest of the season to hunt.

18

The Manzes

NOT ONLY WAS JIM AN EXCEPTIONAL HUNTER, but he was a supurb woodsman as well. He had hunted those woods for miles around and never bothered with a compass. He simply knew every ridge, slough, and tall pine by memory. He would hunt the entire season, always walking and enjoying the woods in the process. His boys were brought up the same way. They seldom waited on a stand. They preferred stalking deer and became good shots.

In 1964, I took my brother-in-law Gerald to Park Rapids for his first deer hunt, planning to hunt by the "Ranch." About two years earlier, Harold Manz had purchased an old deer hunting cabin and some land by a small lake where I had taken Woody and Burt fishing. It was only about three miles from the Ranch. They invited me to hunt with them, but I enjoyed the Ranch, I had a large area to hunt, and I seldom saw a hunter from another party, and Jim was always helpful in trying to fill tags.

Getting to the woods early, we decided to visit the Manzes before going to the meadow. Harold asked us to hunt with them, and we thought it would be fun to hunt with them that morning. We entered the woods before daylight, using flashlights to find our way. We were on the north end of the lake and would be hunting to the northeast. A short way into the woods, they dropped me off by what they called "the raspberry patch," and then took Gerald further into the woods along a narrow foot trail.

Bigger Yet

I WAS STANDING ON THE SOUTH EDGE of a small grassy area—"the raspberry patch"—with a creek to my left and woods and brush to the northeast and south. It was about an hour after sun up when a deer came running in from the east and abruptly stopped in thick brush north of the patch. It appeared to have been spooked and was seeking safety in the brush. I couldn't see its body, only a huge rack in the brush. It soon began twisting its head back and forth, apparently having caught my scent.

Knowing I wouldn't have much time before the deer would bolt, I had to shoot quickly. From the disturbance in the brush, I judged where the head should be and fired. At the shot, all went silent and the rack disappeared. I was confused. In about ten seconds, I again heard a rustle in the brush and the buck rushed back to the east the way he had come, with his head down. I could see the brush moving but didn't see the deer until it crossed the narrow trail. I took a quick shot. The woods again went silent.

I assumed the buck had escaped into the woods. Walking down the trail toward where I had seen it last, I wasn't particularly hopeful, but I had a big surprise. A beautiful buck lay across the trail, but I could find no mark on its body. Poking it with the gun barrel, I got no reaction from the deer. It was dead, but I couldn't see where it was hit. Then I saw a drop of blood rise out of the hair on its neck.

Later, looking at the rack, the tip of one of its center tines had been broken off by my first shot. The bullet had hit the taller tine, and it had fragmented. I found bits of lead embedded in the short tine. It was an eleven pointer with a heavy rack, the largest deer I had shot.

136

Manzes skinning a deer.

Manz's DeerCamp, 2008.

This was the only deer our party got that day, but Gerald had missed a doe.

They invited us to stay over, and we enjoyed the camp life and companionship of other hunters.

The next morning, I walked out early, but in the semi-darkness, I caught a branch across my right eye as I went down the trail. It really hurt, and, afterwards, I just couldn't keep that eye opened. And, as I couldn't see out of my right eye, that also affected my left. I continued on because I didn't think the problem would last.

A little later, a doe appeared in front of me, standing broadside about thirty yards away. I could still aim with my left eye, but it was watering so badly I couldn't see the front sight. I didn't take a shot. This pointed up to me how important it was to wear some type of eye protection when walking through brush, especially in the dark and semi-dark of early morning.

I went to the doctor, and he put a patch on the eye that I had to wear for a week.

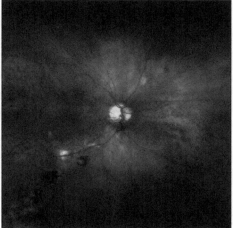

Author's Note: About thirty years ago, I began to need greater eye care, and in checking my eyes, the doctor found a serious scar on my right cornea. He, of course, asked what had caused it, and I didn't know. Not, that is, until I started writing this book and remembered this incident.

The next year, I went hunting the Ranch with Gerald, as Jim was in another area half a mile to the east. They knew the area for miles around and would usually choose a new area each day to hunt. On average, we would get more deer per day, but they had the whole season to hunt. It was their vacation, and their hunting required more skill. Having no luck by noon, I met Gerald and another hunter in the meadow. I decided to put them on a stand while I made a short drive from the south side of the meadow. I told them where they should stand, and I went to make the drive.

I had just started my drive, walking around a small brush area, when my eyes and those of a doe met at the same time. We were about forty yards apart. She had been looking ahead, but as she noticed me, her head jerked towards me, and in a split second she was off and running.

I was fortunate that my gun fit me well because I don't believe I aimed, just pointed it, like with my shot gun. At the second shot, the deer fell, having run only about thirty feet. It was hit in the chest, but with two holes on one side and one on the other. My second shot had entered or exited one of the holes of my first shot.

Going up to Gerald and the other hunters, they were not where I had expected them to be. The doe would have gone past them.

This was my first deer not gotten while still hunting or being in a stand, that is, other than my lucky first deer.

Who Needs Skill?

THE NEXT YEAR, GERALD WAS GOING into the service on the Monday after the deer opener, so we brought a camper so we could stay overnight, to give him two days of hunting. I also invited another hunter whom I had met in Jaycees. Don was an experienced hunter.

A beautiful light snow, about four inches, had fallen overnight, giving us great visibility and showing tracks of any deer in the area. Gerald decided to hunt the meadow, and Don and I walked deeper into the woods towards the northeast.

Gerald saw five deer run across the meadow, but they were too far for a shot. Don and I saw no deer, but we did see a few fresh tracks. The tracks of two deer crossed the trail near a tall pine. It was a great location. To the east was brush with a large hill to the southeast and a big slough to my west. A beautiful ridge line of birch and popple rose on the west and north side. I would have shooting of up to 150 yards across the slough.

The next morning, Gerald went back to the meadow, Don headed further to the north, and I went to that big pine tree. The first limbs started about five feet from the ground, and it was a struggle getting up into the tree with my rifle. From there I climbed about twelve feet up, where I found some branches where I could set fairly comfortably. I even had a limb as a footrest. From my perch, I would be able to shoot to the west and north with a little maneuvering, but not to the east or south.

About 8:30, I noticed a deer walking toward the east, in the birch trees and brush on the north side of the slough. I momentarily lost sight of the animal in the brush, but then spotted its head looking to the west. I could make out the white of the ears, eye, and around the nose, but I saw no part of its body.

Not being experienced with the rifle with its open sights, looking at a 140-yard shot, and trying to balance on tree limbs, I didn't want to try a head shot. I wanted a larger target, the chest. The deer had been walking east, and, with nothing to scare it, I assumed it was looking back over its shoulder. I decided to shoot ahead of and below its nose, where I assumed the chest would be. I would rather have a clean miss than a crippled deer.

At the shot, the deer bolted and ran toward the east, disappearing into the brush. This was one of those interesting moments that occur while deer hunting. Had I done the right thing? Had I hit the deer?

Waiting a few minutes before climbing down from my pine tree and going to the spot where I had seen that deer's head, I found blood. Okay, I'd guessed correctly. The deer had been looking over its shoulder. I found the blood trail and began following it, but I didn't have to go far. She lay just seventy-five feet away, shot in the lung. I dragged her back to the pine tree and left her at the base as I climbed back up into those branches. It was only 10:00.

About half an hour later, a doe came from the west, walking in the heavy brush along the south edge of the slough. It was exciting watching it mosey towards me, but it was moving through brush too thick for me to get a shot. At thirty yards away, my height in the tree gave me the ability to look down into the brush, and I had an easy shot.

Hearing my second shot, Don came to check the action and helped me drag my second deer to the base of the pine tree. I then suggested he take the pine and I would hunt to the north.

About an hour later, when I returned to the tree, Don was cold and wanted out of the pine. He hadn't enjoyed sitting in the tree. Without movement, the cold of the day had seeped into his clothing. He decided to go to a stand closer to the meadow.

I resumed my place in the pine. Less than an hour later, I saw some brown movement in the brush at the northwest corner of the slough, moving to the south. It moved in and out of the trees and brush along the slough. By the time I had adjusted my body to the tree limbs to allow me to position for the shot, the deer had paused with its head and front shoulders behind another large pine and with thick brush ahead of it.

Knowing the deer would soon move, and if it did, I'd lose any chance at a shot, I shot quickly, aiming at what I hoped was the rear of the lungs, just six inches out from the pine shielding it.

At the shot, it appeared the back legs jerked up toward the body, indicating it was hit. Then the deer disappeared into the brush. Again I had those anxious moments. Should I have fired? Did I do the right thing, gotten off a decent kill shot, or had I wounded the animal, possibly crippled it? Knowing I might have hit it in the stomach, I looked at my watch and decided to wait forty-five minutes before climbing down. It would take me about fifteen minutes to reach the spot where the deer had been, that meant I'd have waited an hour.

Finally, climbing down and walking to the corner of the slough where the big pine stood and the deer had been when I shot, I found a maze of tracks going in all directions in the snow. As this was a new snow, that meant a lot of deer had passed through this area. Clearly the deer were on the move. I could find no blood. I knew that if I were more experienced, I might be able to find hair or blood specks and maybe pick up the correct set of tracks.

I began walking to the south, along the edge of the slough and the base of the ridge, seeing many tracks in both directions. After fifty to sixty yards, I noticed something dark about 100 yards ahead of me in the slough. Thinking it could be the deer, I inched ahead, slowing gaining height on the ridge as I did so. That would give me a better view into the slough. With my eyes glued to the dark spot in the cattails and having progressed only twenty yards, I head a muffled sound higher on the ridge.

Looking over my shoulder, I saw a buck lying on the ground, staring lifelessly at me. I had guessed right on my shot and had given him enough time to bed down. I believe it had been following my earlier doe, and the doe had been looking back at him when I shot her.

Before I had the deer dressed, Gerald arrived from the meadow. He had again seen nothing and was excited and awed about my many shots. He helped drag the deer back to the pine tree. I got this idea and said, "Let's play a trick on Don."

I knew he was hunting along the trail we'd have to drag the deer to get to the car. We dragged the buck to his stand and asked him to help drag it back to the car so I could go back for the other doe. Don grabbed the rack with Gerald and took about three steps. He stopped and stared at the buck, then up at me. "You shot three!" I gave the buck to Don.

Don lived with his parents, and Gerald was going into the service the next day. We hung the deer in my garage. Being too frugal to want to pay to have my deer processed, I had two deer skinned, boned and cut up by Tuesday evening. Don hadn't called, so on Wednesday evening, I started skinning his deer. I then thought, why should I process his deer, he has more time than I do? I called Don's parents, asking that he pick up the deer. His dad told me he couldn't, that Don was back up north hunting until late Sunday. I said that the deer was going to rot if it wasn't processed. His dad picked it up.

I took our boned meat to a locker plant to have some ground and some made into sausage. They weighed my meat at ninety-six pounds.

A few weeks later, the locker called back to have me pick up my burgers and sausage. I had a little over ninety pounds of meat, including the added pork used to make the sausage. That seemed strange. I asked why I shouldn't be getting more than my ninety-six pounds rather than less. They said that smoking reduces the weight some. Then they said they had started with eighty-three pounds of boned meat. What? I went in and showed them the slip which clearly noted that I had left ninety-six pounds of meat with them. After a verbal battle, I left, telling them I'd never use their locker again, nor step into their store.

In those days, it was common to "come up short" as many butchers would acquire some venison to add to their ground-up sausage mix and add them to their over-the-counter sales. We were at my wife's parents' house one evening when her mother served ring baloney from a local meat market. My wife, whose sense of taste is very sensitive, was about to take a bite of baloney, when I saw my mother-in-law watching her closely. My wife tasted the meat and looked up at her mother, saying, "There's venison in this baloney."

Her mother had purchased three rings and had tasted vension in the first ring. It had made her wonder.

We were out several weeks later and again had baloney. My wife took one bite and looked up at her mom. They both laughed. It had venison in it too.

Ron's New Adventures

THE NEXT YEAR, I TOOK RON WITH ME on his first deer hunt. We had fished and hunted together for over fifteen years. We had spent every weekend during the pheasant season together hunting. Don was also with us as we were friends in Jaycees. We were both excited when Ron took me up on my offer to take him deer hunting.

The only gun Ron had that he could use for deer hunting was a Japanese rifle given to him by a cousin and manufactured close to the end of World War II. Before he could bring it into the field, he had to take it to a gunsmith, who took the bayonet off, put a bolt through the stock in order to hold it together and fixed him up with a box of shells. It was a right-handed rifle with a peep sight. Ron was left handed. But he didn't want to invest in deer hunting equipment until he had decided if he liked it and would continue to hunt deer.

He wore a pair of flight boots also given to him by a cousin and a pair of flight pants. These were not made for walking, but rather for flyers who flew or rode in the World War II bombers six miles up and in temperatures that would drop to fifty below zero. He would most certainly be warm. For a coat, he had a parka borrowed from his brother, who had been in the navy. All told, Ron was a pretty sorry sight, but I kept my comments mostly to myself.

He went to the shooting range with a cousin to "zero in" the rifle. They shot from a railroad boxcar, and the boom was frightening, he told me. He was far from sure he was going to like this form of hunting. And the rifle was baulky. On the second shot, the trigger was harder to pull, so he assumed he had flipped the safety on. He hadn't. He laid the gun on the table and took hold of the safety bolt to give it a push in, but when he started to push the bolt, the gun fired, and the recoil about tore his thumb off. This made him a bit leery of his gun. Still, he showed up, and we set off.

We approached the area where we were going to hunt late at night and set up the tent camper in the dark. That night the temperature plummeted to thirteen below, which was a record low for the opening of deer season. Ron had a catalytic heater, but it hardly made a dent in the temperature of the camper. By morning, the thermometer, set only one foot away from the heater, read ten above zero. Most of us were chilled to the bone. Ron, however, besides his heavy flight geer, had slept inside two sleeping bags and woke warm as toast. Maybe his get up wasn't as outlandish as I had thought.

We woke at an ungodly hour when, according to Ron, pheasants would still be in dreamland, had a bit to eat, dressed and were ready to hit the trail. I took Ron under my wing as we walked out to where we would hunt. Ron was dressed so warmly that he actually began to perspire and his glasses fogged up, but he seemed to be able to follow me as I crashed through the frosty brush.

I finally stopped and told Ron to walk for a while, then climb a tree. Looking at his cumbersome clothing, I wondered how that would go. I told him to try to stay in his tree for a couple of hours then head back to the trail and the camper.

That evening as we warmed up and ate our supper, I asked Ron how he liked deer hunting. He said, "I'd nearly froze to death and I saw absolutely nothing, no deer. Not even a bird."

The next morning the weather had warmed considerably. I took Ron to my stand, a large pine tree with branches like a ladder. I suggest he walk several blocks further and maybe just stand by the base of a tree, keep his eyes open and stay as quiet and motionless as possible. I suggested he come back to my stand after maybe two hours.

After two hours, Ron came back to my tree, having seen nothing. I had him climb up into my pine while I would make a loop around the area. Walking was much more comfortable this morning, and the sun was up. I started my loop. About halfway around, I heard a huge explosion—Ron's ancient rifle—and headed back to see what had happened. When I reached Ron, he was just climbing down from the big pine. He told me what had happened.

"I saw a coyote first and put my sights on him. I thought about shooting him, but I figured you'd get on my case for scaring away the deer. Then I heard a branch snap. I looked in that direction and saw an eight-point buck emerge from a grove of popple trees that were almost as white as birch. Now I was really excited, and I worried that the deer could hear my heart thumping. With every step the buck was getting closer. I pulled off my gloves and managed to get the rifle off safe without it going off.

"But I didn't know how to shot the deer. It was coming towards me, never giving me a side shot. I didn't know how to shot a deer coming at me. Just as it was going to pass the tree, I had to shoot. That's the explosion you heard.

I attempted to eject the shell and get a new one into the barrel, but the rifle was giving me trouble. The deer was fleeing. Finally, I got the shell in and was going to take a second shot, but that's when I saw the deer slow down, stop. Its legs shook a moment, and then it just toppled over."

Ron and I headed to the deer and discovered his buck. Ron had shot it right through the heart.

"I had no idea a deer could run seventy-five yards with a hole in its heart," Ron said.

That night in camp, Don told us he hadn't seen a deer. Only Ron had. He wore a very big smile.

Getting that one deer, we decided to go back the next Saturday but not stay overnight.

We left St. Cloud about 1:00 a.m. and got to the meadow well before sunup. We walked out into the woods with flashlights. I put Don on a stand before we came to my pine tree.

There was some old snow on the ground but some new hoar frost on top of that would help us spot fresh deer tracks. Nearing my pine, I spotted two sets of fresh tracks. They had crossed our trail, heading toward the east, through some brush and over a ridge overlooking a large slough. The slough was surrounded by hills with heavy woods and brush.

I told Ron to go ahead to the northwest corner of the slough and to pick a stand there, and I would track the deer, hoping to drive them toward him when it got light.

Giving him time to get set, I began my stalk through the heavy head-high brush. I had just gotten to the top of the ridge overlooking the slough when I heard, then saw, a deer running along the ridge up on the right side of the slough. It was a tough shot as I had to stand on my tiptoes and raise my rifle above my shoulder to get off a shot above the brush. At the shot, the deer dropped and began thrashing around. Looking to my left, I saw a second deer disappear over the ridge on the east side of the slough.

I got to the deer I had hit. It was a doe with a wound in its neck and it was still flailing wildly. Not wanting to scare other deer with a second shot—and being generally a frugal person—I found a broken tree limb and clubbed it. Half an hour later, I had field dressed the animal, and I stood up to scan the slough. And where I had seen the second deer disappear over the ridge, I heard the breaking of brush. Then a large buck broke out of the brush to my left almost exactly where I had first jumped the deer.

The buck ran across the slough, and I opened up. I believe my 30-30 held seven shells, and I was down to my last shot, when the buck slowed down to turn as it entered the brush. I took time to aim and fired the last shell. The deer dropped at about 200 yards.

It was one of the largest deer I had ever shot, and I discovered one of its hind legs had a large "club foot," probably developed after it had broken its foot.

I believe the buck had been with the doe and had somehow snuck around he far side of the slough to get back with her, trying to find where they had parted so he could follow her.

I enjoyed meat that was more tender than what a mature buck would have, so I offered Don the buck or the doe, but I told him if he took the buck, I wanted the rack. He took the buck. Don said later that, after hanging six days, the buck weighed 206 pounds. That was a heavy deer for the north woods. I never got my rack.

New Area

There were now more hunters hunting off the Ranch, and trails going in many directions, so the next fall I explored the area further to the north of the meadow. I found a beautiful small deep slough with a huge beaver lodge on the west side. The lodge had been enlarged by generations of beavers and is still in use today, some forty years after I first saw it.

There was a shorter walk to an old logging road to the east, but I saw some stands as I neared the road. It seemed convenient, but also would allow other hunters to follow us in. I decided it was better to come off the meadow and have more privacy.

The first few hundred yards off the meadow were easy, but then it got difficult finding a way in the dark, especially since we didn't want a defined trail. With heavy brush and many small sloughs, we understood why others were not in this area. It would be a nightmare in the dark.

I decided to mark a few larger trees that gave me directions I could follow with a flashlight. I broke some green brush to indicate trail directions too. In breaking and bending brush in the direction we would be walking in the morning, we exposed some inner wood that would shine under the beam of a flashlight.

That fall we decided to hunt west and north of the beaver pond and at the end of the two smaller sloughs north of the pond. The trail north of the pond required more trail marking as it was an area of thick brush with detours around the sloughs.

I put Ron on a stand near the pond. Don went to the west, and I went to the north, trying to follow our new trail. Coming back to Ron about noon, neither of us had seen a deer, though we both had heard one close shot. It might have been Don.

I suggested Ron go to the north to the end of the sloughs, and I would take his stand by the pond.

As the white of the broken brush would not be visible returning, I told Ron to start back before sunset and stop by my stand. If we allowed half an hour of light from that point, we would have light enough to walk out. Don planned to take a short cut and meet us at the cars.

It was a quiet afternoon, and I heard no shots anywhere close. It was cold, so I was anxious to leave by sunset. About 5:00, pretty much as I was thinking about leaving, I heard a branch snap in the woods to the west, and I assumed it was a deer trying to sneak by me.

It was past the time Ron should have been coming back, and I was getting concerned. A few minutes later I heard a voice far to the north. In the cold, crisp air, voices could travel a great distance. I worried that Ron was having a problem finding his way back. Setting aside my rifle, I grabbed my flashlight and rushed up the trail. I could make out some of the broken branches in the dim light, but occasionally I had to use the flashlight to make my way.

Getting to Ron's stand, I found it empty. It was nearing full dark by now, and with a cloud cover, it was getting really dark. My flashlight was losing power too and was of little use as its batteries died. I tried to find my way by memory but occasionally had to turn and try to light up some of those broken branches to make sure I was on track. I often had to walk sideways to pick up the glow of the inner wood behind me.

I finally made it back to the pond, and the batteries were completely dead. Again no sign of Ron. I had a florescent compass pinned to my coat, so I decided to work my way to the south where I would either hit a trail or reach the meadow. With a visibility of about twenty feet, I was breaking through a lot of brush. After about 200 feet, I stopped to check my direction. My compass was gone, torn off by the brush.

Lost?

I WAS ON THE EDGE OF A SMALL SLOUGH. With no sense of direction, I decided to set up there for the night. I found a blown over tree I used for a bench and back rest and cleared a spot for a fire. There were scattered areas of melting snow, so I had no concern about a leaf or grass fire, but, at the same time, the wood was wet.

Laying aside my gun, my remaining food and flashlight, I went searching to find some birch bark or popple bark to start a fire, but my search around the slough revealed no starter bark, and I didn't dare to wander far from my camp. I laid some branches in a straight line on the ground to find my way back once I reached some dry tinder, and I finally was able to find some tinder bark about 100 feet from my impromptu camp. With a small fire started, the flames acted as a beacon and I was able to go further out in search of dry wood and tinder.

I was excited about staying in the woods overnight, but concerned at the same time. With the temperature now at freezing, I was glad for a warm fire. With that fire as the center of my world, I scoured the woods around it for a large supply of somewhat dry wood and laid it over the fire to dry. I found a few heavy limbs that would last me most of the night.

For food, I had some cheese sandwiches, which tasted mighty fine as I ate them next to my fire. I could use snow for water, so I was set.

In the meantime, Ron had left the woods before sunset as he was supposed to, but, instead of walking to my stand, he had gone to the west, hoping to scare up a deer or drive one to me. He was the one I had heard breaking a branch. He finally reached the cars, and Don was waiting. We had planned to stay overnight and had left our camper at Val Chatel, about a mile to the west. Figuring I would be out soon, they decided to take Ron's car and go back to the camper to start supper.

As for me, it was 6:30, dark, and there was no sign of Ron or Don, but I was enjoying my outing. Then I thought that maybe I should make a hunter's sign of distress, three evenly spaced rifle shots into the air. Even in the tent camper, they should be able to hear those reports in a still, cold night. And they did. They were also sure it was me. They also figured I had broken my leg or had some other catastrophe.

Rushing back to the meadow, they stopped by the hunters in the ranch house, asking if they had seen me and if they'd be willing to form a search party if they weren't back by 9:00.

In the meantime, I had collected a large amount of birch bark, just in case my fire went out and I had to start a new fire, and enough wood to last the night. I heard a noise and listened. A grouse. This was the first time I had ever heard a grouse drum at night. It was a beautiful sound.

I sat back against the tree, enjoying the quiet of the still evening. This was the kind of peaceful adventure one only dreams about, yet I was having it. I felt very fortunate. Hunters forced to stay out overnight in cold weather were often not nearly so lucky.

About 8:30, I heard some distant yelling coming from the south. I listened but couldn't make anything out. Then I caught the flicker of a flashlight bouncing through the woods. Both the yelling and the lights—two of them—were coming nearer.

I threw all the birch bark into the fire, making a snapping fire ball that nearly blinded me. While I was trying to get my eyes adjusted, Ron rushed up, looking worried, probably thinking he'd find me in agony and in need of some kind of helicopter lift out. Nope.

As they calmed down, I gathered up my gear and prepared to kill the fire. The walk out was somewhat anti-climatic, especially for those expecting to be heroes rescuing a fellow hunter in grave distress.

Back at the camper, Don announced that he had see Blacky. Ron and I both thought we knew what he meant, but we asked anyway.

"A black bear," he said.

Black bears certainly were around in these woods, though I had never seen one while deer hunting, and they were legal to shoot if one had a deer license. We asked Don if he had taken a shot. He said, "No, I don't believe in shooting bear."

Ron and I were a little upset as we were hunting as a party, sharing our success equally, and a bear would have been a most valuable hunting trophy.

He said he had been hunting on the south side of a hill, with a grass slough below it. The bear had come from the east and walked around the south side of the slough. Don described its progress as a sort of bouncing gait as it continued to the west.

We had heard a shot coming from Don's general direction earlier in the day, but he said it wasn't him. We had known there were hunters to the north of us, but none to the west.

The next day, Don hunted a different area, and Ron walked back to where Don had been hunting the day before. Again we had a heavy frost on the ground but only scattered spots of snow. Tracking should be decent.

Walking back to the east side of the slough, Ron saw a light blood trail, made more visible with the frost. The blood trail continued along the south side of the slough, going to the west toward Val Chatel, and our camper. Ron mentioned this to me, but not to Don.

Ron and I returned to the meadow the next weekend, but not with Don. We met our friend Bob. He was still hunting and attempted to drive deer to us. We mentioned the bear, and Bob had some interesting information. The previous Sunday afternoon, as guests were sitting in the Val Chatel restaurant, a bear appeared on the ski hill dragging its hind quarters. The owner, Rod Peterson, called Bob, who was a good friend and had worked with Rod, asking him to get some hunters and pursue the bear. It took them only a short time to track it down. They found the bear in some brush. It had been shot in the right hindquarters. After the hunters dispatched the poor animal, they dug out the spent bullet from the hindquarters. It was the same caliber as Don's rifle.

No one claimed shooting at a bear, and it would have been big news for someone to bag one as bears were rarely seen or shot during deer hunting. Jim had only shot one in his many years of hunting.

This was the last year we hunted with Don. Despite his years of experience, he never shot a deer when he was with us.

152

19

Hunting with Lowell

Rut-Stupid

THE NEXT YEAR, RON—NOW FIRMLY HOOKED to deer hunting—hunted on the west side of the pond. A buck walked by and stopped to stare at him. He shot, and the deer ran about fifty yards, stopped, turned around and came back to stare at him again. The first shot would have been fatal, given a bit more time, but the second was instantly successful. When Ron told me about this animal's strange behavior, I just shrugged. When in rut, bucks sometimes did some very strange things.

Ron had several boys, and, as they grew older, we began to hunt with our own families, but we still got together on a regular basis.

Quick Learner

I HAD EXPOSED MY SON LOWELL to the excitement of the woods, and he soon became more familiar with the woods than I was. He had a knack for identifying the few pine trees and remembering each ridge and slough. He had developed many of the woods skills of Jim's boys.

His first deer hunting trip was when he was eleven, and we brought up some friends from church. We stayed in a tent camper. It was near the end of November, in about 1976, and my coldest deer hunt. The thermometer read twenty-nine below zero on Saturday morning and thirty-one below on Sunday morning. These were very cold temperatures for a trip in the tent camper. We were at least fortunate that, in very cold weather, there is less wind. But the deer weren't moving, and we got together in the afternoon to make a drive. With the day temperature at fourteen below, it was a cold drive.

I had purchased a Remington 30-06 automatic, and Lowell had my 30-30. While waiting for the drive to begin, Lowell put his tongue on the magazine of his rifle. He had been told that this was a very bad idea, and maybe that's why he had to try it. He immediately learned just exactly why one should never do this. He had to mumble to get our attention, and we quickly saw his plight. I'll give him credit though, because he didn't compound his situation by getting his lips attached to the metal as well. I could see the panic in his eyes as he tried to pull his tongue loose from the magazine. It was stuck fast.

One of my friends quickly said, "Let's breathe on the metal and warm it up."

It took a while, but we finally got Lowell's tongue free. Despite the pain he had to be feeling, he did not complain. I could see, however, that he had difficult time eating for a few days.

There were six of us in the group, but because of the cold and little deer movement, two went home on Saturday night. And late that afternoon Lowell had developed a bad case of the croup, which certainly did not help when we wanted to stay as quiet as possible. The two hunters who wanted to go home wanted to take Lowell back with them, but Lowell insisted on staying. We slept that night in double sleeping bags, and in the morning he was better, and that made him happy.

As we were using a tent camper, we had both the small furnace and the two-burner stove with us and on, but with the propane jelling up, there was little flame and not a lot of heat. We had brought along orange juice, but by morning there were two inches of ice on all sides of the container.

In a Pine Tree at 31° Below

At thirty-one below, we decided to hunt until 10:00, and then determine what to do. I went to my pine tree and let Lowell walk around in the woods to help keep him warm. Today's cold-weather gear far outstrips what we had in 1976, and all of us were mindful of the necessity to pay attention and not take frostbite lightly.

After the first few years of hunting that area, I had found a better location in the pine, up about twenty-eight feet. I could see over some of the closer brush and also down into it. It was less comfortable sitting on smaller limbs than my lower position, but the loss of comfort was more than made up by the better view. In the deep cold, there was little to no wind, and I decided to see how long I could tolerate the cold sitting still in the tree. One hour and four minutes. Then I just had to come down and get moving or risk frostbite.

I heard Lowell shoot, and a little later I saw him coming through the woods with his rifle in his left hand. Through the brush I saw something being held over his right shoulder, but it looked like a large feather next to his head. I had no idea what he was bringing back. When he reached the bottom of my pine, I could see it was a porcupine tail.

I had always taught Lowell that whatever we shoot, we eat, but I had never heard of anyone eating a porcupine—not by choice anyway—so what was I to do?

When Lowell lifted the porky off his back, his wool cap came along with it, as quills were imbedded in it. Lowell was proud of his quarry. I had no choice then. I had eaten muskrat, woodchuck, raccoon, beaver, along with a multitude of other animals, so why not porcupine. But that wasn't the first problem. Just touching the ends of those barbed quills risked getting them stuck in fingers. How would we skin the animal? Turning it over, however, we found that there were no quills on the stomach, so I sliced the skin there and shucked out the body from its skin. Truthfully, it was an ugly looking carcass, and working in that kind of cold hurt our hands, but we were thankful for the warmth of the porcupine's body.

When we brought home Lowell's catch, my wife wasn't happy, but by using her favorite "celery soup," the porky tasted just fine.

A few years later I took two porcupines to a church wild game feed, and it was a hit. The next year people asked why I didn't bring them again.

Anyway, on that cold, cold weekend, we saw no deer and went home early. Hunting was slow, but Lowell got his first deer hunting experience and, despite the problems, he enjoyed it.

That year we had begun construction of deer stands to be more comfortable, and we ended out making a row of stands west of the pond over the next two years. I put Lowell in a stand on a hill, and I walked down a swale to a tree overlooking a slough. It was a good location, but there was only a single elm tree and it didn't have the support structure to support a stand. It was not comfortable to sit on a single limb, but I had a good view over the slough. We had a good snow cover that year too. About mid-morning, a buck came running along the edge of the slough from the west. I had to struggle to get my only shot but it was from a very awkward position. The deer showed no sign of being hit and continued to run in Lowell's direction, disappearing over a small knoll.

I climbed down and checked the tracks. As the snow made for good tracking, I followed the deer for a third of a mile as it had turned to the left away from Lowell. I saw no blood.

I returned to my elm, lamenting, as all hunters do from time to time, why did I miss? After another hour, I walked back toward Lowell. This time, I found more fresh tracks and blood. The buck had followed our morning tracks for a few yards, then turned into some heavy brush

156

and died. Lowell had seen it coming, but it turned aside before it came into range and disappeared.

I realized what had happened. I had been tracking another set of fresh tracks, missing completely the ones of the buck I had shot at. I had made the mistake of not going to the place where I thought I had hit the deer and tracking from there. As I followed the correct trail, I still saw no blood for about fifty yards.

Lowell finally got his first deer, of many, at the age of sixteen. He was hunting south of the pond, and I heard him shoot twice, then a third shot a little later. Walking down to where he was, I saw that he had gotten a nice buck, but he looked a little disheveled. His first shot had taken out the deer's shoulder, and the second hit the spine, dropping the deer. But the deer was still struggling. Not wanting to shoot it again like the old man, he decided to cut its throat. He locked the good leg behind the rack and mounted the deer. As he started to cut the throat, the deer balked and bucked him off. He then figured he'd better just shoot it.

As a group of five or six hunters, we would usually go up Friday evening or early Saturday morning, hunt until Sunday noon, and then pack up. We usually hunted the string of stands west of the pond. I usually took the first stand, and Lowell the last one. He would walk with the guys and assign them a stand as they made their way down the line. He could manage the dark very well, so no one got lost.

I would have everyone stay in their stand until about 9:00. Then we would walk a while to warm up and get back in the stands about 9:30. At 10:00 I would begin a drive, circling in from the north and driving the deer toward the stands.

There were other hunters further to the north of us, hunting off the road, and they often ended up chasing deer into the dead zone between us. We usually got one deer per drive.

Didn't Give Up

THIS YEAR THE HUNTING GROUP INCLUDED DAVE, Verne, Lowell, his friend Pat, and me. In the morning I had heard shots to the west, and I was pretty sure it was from our group. I began my drive at 10:00 as we had arranged and drove an eight-point buck to the middle of the stands. I reached Lowell's stand at about 11:00, and he said he had gotten a spike buck, and Dave, hunting next to him, had shot at another buck, but it had raced west out of our area. This had occurred even before my drive, and Lowell had helped Dave find a light blood trail. He would try to track down the deer after the drive.

I went to the south, planning to make another circle and drive the deer from the south. Lowell took the opportunity to track Dave's deer.

After about 100 yards, a doe came racing towards me from the south, apparently kicked up by Jim's group. This gave us three deer.

A little while later, I heard a shot from west of Lowell's stand, and I hoped they had gotten Dave's deer. Meeting up with Lowell at 2:00, he said I wouldn't believe where Dave had hit his deer—in one testical. With no snow and very little blood, he had trouble with the trail, often losing it. He had to follow part of the way by instinct and disturbed leaves. The deer had bedded down, and Lowell was able to sneak up on it and got it just as it jumped up.

A few minutes later, Bob came in from the west. He knew where Lowell's stand was and had driven the spike buck to him earlier that morning, and possibly the one that ran towards me. Lowell gave Bob the deer, as they were 0 for 4.

On Sunday morning, Dave had again hit a deer, leaving a blood trail towards the meadow. He and another hunter followed it, but had given up, as it was nearly noon. They hadn't given the deer time to lay down, and, as it was Sunday, they wanted to leave.

Lowell, Pat, and I decided to stay, wait a couple of hours, and then try to track the deer down. We weren't accustomed to leaving a crippled deer behind if we could possibly help it.

158

At 3:30, we began to track the deer. I followed the trail with them out on the side. After a short distance, I heard the sound of small branches breaking. By the muffled sound of the branches, I thought it might be that a deer had lay down on them. I got the attention of Lowell and Pat, and we backtracked.

I told them I thought the deer was lying down in a small patch of brush. There was no snow, and if the deer ran, there would be little or no blood after lying down so long. As Lowell was a better tracker, I suggested he go after the deer, and Pat and I would circle, pick a stand on the far side where we expected the deer might run.

Making a wide circle, we were on our stands for half an hour, but we had heard no sound. We called to Lowell, but he made no reply. Walking back to where I expected him to be, we found nothing. I decided we should go back to the stands and wait.

About 4:30, we heard a shot from near the meadow, over half a mile away, and a few minutes later a second shot.

By now it was past sundown, and we were wondering what to do. Then we heard three horn honks from the east, where we had parked.

Rushing back to the cars, we found Lowell standing by the truck, looking sweaty and tired. We asked him if he'd seen the deer.

"Yep."

"Did you shoot it?"

"Look in the back of the truck."

We did. A nice six-point buck lay in the bed of the truck. As we examined it, we saw that Dave had hit it in the lower left leg. This was a wound that still gave the deer three legs. A deer could move a long ways with three legs. These leg-hit deer were seldom recovered.

Lowell had followed the deer almost all the way to the meadows and dragged it back on one of the gravel trails. It was over a mile-long drag. He had jumped the deer from its bed, but he couldn't get off a shot. It had apparently run before we got to our stands. There was no blood, so he had to follow the deer more by sound and instinct. Still in his teens, he had developed great ability to track and had a wonderful instinct about where a deer would go if wounded.

Following those instincts, he had jumped the deer a second time, again watching it bound away into the woods without being able to get off a shot. But he realized that the deer hadn't run very far between the two sightings. He was especially quiet and cautious as he followed the deer, jumping it a third time. He was able to get off a shot that caught the deer in the jaw, stunning it. He then put a second shot.

Pastor's First Deer

THE NEXT YEAR WE TOOK OUR PASTOR on his first deer hunt, and also two other church members. My cousin Wayne also came to join us at 5:00 a.m., as we were about to enter the woods. It was again a difficult year to hunt, with no snow and noisy dry leaves.

Lowell was the first to spot a deer, but after taking a shot could find no evidence of the deer being hit. After a long search, he saw a "strange white" in some grass and leaves. It was his doe.

I put the pastor in the elm tree where I had taken the deer that ran towards Lowell. It wasn't a comfortable stand, but it was certainly a good location. I told him I would make a drive after sun up, so he wouldn't have to sit too long.

Shortly after I started my drive, I heard him shoot. Going to his stand, he told me two deer had come by, and he had gotten off a shot at the second one. He said the deer had been about thirty yards away. He was sure he had hit the deer, but it had run off, and he couldn't find it. He sounded very confident that he had hit the deer, and I suggested we have Lowell help us search for it at noon.

With Lowell's help, we searched for an hour, and finally gave up. Walking back to the stand, Lowell was still searching the landscape. He suddenly said, "There it is," and pointed into the woods.

We looked but couldn't see anything. He said, "Can't you see its ear and its eye in the leaves behind that tree?"

It was a fawn, but the pastor thought it was a big deer. We agreed for his sake that it was an "adult fawn."

Near sundown, Wayne also shot at a deer, thought he hit it, but couldn't find it. He had to go back that night, so we said Lowell would look for it the next day. Yes, Lowell found that one, too, his "third" impossible find in two days.

We always seemed to have excellent luck, with Jim and his boys helping us from the south and the road hunters from the east and north. Most of our deer were easy shots, just nosing through our area. In one two-year period, as a group of six and five, we saw eleven deer, and brought back ten, hunting only a day and a half each year. In an eight-year period, I only saw one strange hunter in our area.

Noon Break

ONE YEAR THERE WERE SIX OF US, including Dave's twin boys on their first deer hunt. The first day, we all got deer except the twins. They had seen some deer, but had never shot a deer rifle before coming up to hunt, and had't gotten off shots. I wanted each of us to get a deer, so the next morning, I took one twin, and Lowell guided the other. We were able to get each of the boys a deer by noon.

One year we were hunting with Dave, Verne, and Ford, and by the first evening we had two deer. Just before dark, Ford had shot at a third deer and had nicked it in the leg and through the udder. It apparently had a late fawn—there was milk on the trail along with blood. Knowing we would have to give it time to lay down, we decided to wait until morning to track it.

Dave and Verne had to go back that night, and Ford had a large Sunday morning paper route, so Lowell and I would be alone the next morning.

Lowell had gone to hunt a new area, by the "rock pond," and I had heard him shoot just before sunset. As the others walked out our trail, I went to meet Lowell. He had gotten off a long shot that afternoon and thought he had hit the deer, but it was getting too late to try to track a deer in the dry leaves.

Taking a short cut to our car, we jumped a deer, but it was too dark to see it. We could tell by the way it ran that it was injured. We heard it run a short distance, then lie down.

Lowell wanted to go after it, but I said we should wait until morning, as it now was very dark, and the deer would likely keep running if we pushed it.

The next morning, with Ford gone on his paper delivery route, Lowell and I went back alone. We had two deer for the five we'd started out with in the group, and we had two cripples to track down.

We both hunted near the beaver pond, and if one of us got a deer, we would then search for the cripples.

I got a spike buck about nine, and Lowell then went to track the deer we had chased up the previous evening. A short time later, I heard a shot, and Lowell soon returned. He had found the deer.

Following Ford's deer to the south, we found where it had laid down, but then gotten back up, heading to the west. We found it lying in the leaves a short distance away.

While dressing that deer, and removing the heart, I felt a weak heart beat. We called Ford to pick up his deer.

Walking across the ice on the pond, one of our party heard a "wup, wup," in the air, and then something hit the ice. Investigating, he found an expended rifle bullet imbedded in the ice. It was from a rifle shot a long distance away.

Tough Drag

We had many more exciting adventures near the pond, but my last hunting trip to Park Rapids was in 1993, just before my first hip replacement. Lowell had left early on Friday morning to meet some of our group and stay over night. I had planned to meet them that evening, but I was delayed by work and decided to head up early in the morning instead and meet them in the woods.

I got to the woods before they had left camp and decided to start in, knowing I would be slowed down by leg pain. There was about twelve inches of fresh snow in the ground, and I took a stand on the west side of the pond, just over the hill.

The rest of the group followed my tracks in a little later and called a quiet hello as they passed by me headed towards their stands to the west.

Luck was with me again. An hour after sunrise, a deer came toward me from the east. It moved along the north side of the pond and crossed the ditch between the beaver pond and the slough to the north and angled to the north, into some thick woods. I would have only one chance at it as it crossed an area of windfalls. At the shot, it disappeared and, but a few seconds later, I saw a flick of its white tail. It was down, and I soon discovered it was a nice six-point buck.

Lowell, Ford, and Bob.

Not wanting to disturb the early morning hunt of the rest of the group, and having work waiting for me at home, I decided to drag the deer out alone. It was difficult dragging it up the hills. I had to do a side-step with my legs, and could only manage about two feet at a time, but the snow made it easier than it could have been.

Change in Terrain

After the hip operation, I thought it best to avoid the long walks in the northwoods, and switched to hunting my wife's parents' farm. It was a difficult change from the solitude of the large woods, having few hunters within half a mile to having them just over the fence line.

My wife's parents had a farm ten miles north of St. Cloud, with cropland, woods, and sloughs on an eighty-acre section of their farm. This time was one of adjustment, and I felt restricted in a small area and surrounded by hunters.

The first year I built a crude stand in the crotch of a tree only to discover that, on opening morning, two hunters had a stand less than 100 yards away.

That was the year I learned patience, as the only deer I saw was shot by another hunter, as it was running towards me.

Since 1994 I've seen a large increase in deer numbers, and I've enjoyed the short walks to a comfortable flat-bottom stand with four-foot walls and a stool.

The next year I shot my first deer with a bit of luck.

There had been a beautiful snowfall, with large fluffy flakes covering the trees and brush and no wind to dislodge it. I was walking back at noon when I noticed a dark shadow behind an area of snow-covered brush. I thought what I was seeing was the head of a deer watching me. With nothing to lose, I shot through the brush where I thought the chest should be. At the shot, the deer bolted into the woods, but it went only about sixty yards.

It looked to be large for a fawn but too small for a doe. A neighboring hunter soon walked over and confirmed it was a fawn. I hadn't realized the crop land fawns were larger than those of the northwoods.

To give my two grandsons—Weston, eight, and Cody, five—their first hunting experience, I called them up and said I needed help dragging a deer out of the woods. I didn't know who enjoyed it more, them pulling, or me watching.

Of the next four deer I shot at, I only hit two. In all my previous years of hunting, I had harvested all but two I'd shot at. It was now more difficult with more running deer.

First Shot "Bull's Eye"

After my record misses, I decided to buy a scope with a wider view. My old scope was thirty-six years old. The first shot I took with the new scope proved a bull's eye, in more ways than one.

My grandson Weston was in high school and working part time. He had to leave for work early, so he hunted with me until 9:00. Going back to his car, he heard some noise in the brush and assumed it was a deer.

A half hour later, I noticed a spike buck trying to sneak by me, and I raised the rifle. He took off running, directly away from me. The new scope gave me a much wider angle and at the first shot, the deer dropped. I was still watching it from my stand when two other hunters walked over to check the action. We walked to the deer together, and all of us looked for a wound. Seeing none, we turned the deer over, and still we found no wound. Bewildered, one of us noticed a drop of blood on the rectum. I had made a perfect bull's eye on that deer as he ran away from me.

I continued to get my deer each year, but lacking some of the previous excitement. That ended in 2007.

Seeing no deer on the first day, I reluctantly went out early on the second. As one gets older, sleep is harder to achieve, and I was a bit tired that second morning. By 9:00 I had seen nothing and heard nothing, but then I caught a flash of white out of the corner of my eye. Quickly turning, the deer had gone, vanished into the brush. But I knew it was there. Then I saw a light-colored leaf flutter in the breeze. I thought maybe that's what my eye had seen, but I wasn't sure.

I then turned my attention in that direction and lay my rifle on the edge of the stand. Twenty minutes later, I had turned to check my back side, and quickly turned back. There was a buck sneaking through the brush. I was fortunate I was holding the rifle, and I only had time for one quick shot. It was a lung shot, and the deer went down about 100 yards away. It is interesting how alert you may have to be to get off a shot.

The next summer, the neighbors built a stand near mine, so I decided to hunt about 300 yards to the east in another of my stands, one I called the canvass stand. It was located it in a narrow band of oak woods with a grass and willow slough thirty yards to the north and a cornfield fifty yards to the south. This stand had been abandoned by hunters many years before.

The first morning the only deer I saw was on the neighbor's land. It was in range, but I didn't shoot as we had respect for each other's property. We were friends and would help each other if help was needed.

With many leaves still on the red oaks, it was already quite dark as it was nearing sundown. But it had been a warm day, and, even though there was little visibility in the woods, I was content to hang over the side of the stand, looking toward the cornfield where there was still some visibility against the light-colored corn stalks.

As it got down to the last few minutes of hunting, half an hour after sundown, I was just sitting there in a daze, bringing back memories of the past and visualizing a deer walking out and standing in the cornfield in front of me.

Suddenly I saw movement on the ground, about fifteen feet from the tree. Coming back to my senses, I saw the outline of a deer. Bringing up the rifle, I knew it was too dark in the woods to see the deer in the scope. Looking down the rifle barrel, I shot at what I thought was the chest. At the shot, the deer raced off to my left. It ran about forty yards, and then all became quiet.

It Only Takes Two Ears

I COULD SEE ONLY THE WHITE OF THE TAIL, so I wondered if it was down or if I should try to shoot again. Suddenly the white of the tail disappeared, and I then saw the white of two ears. I could see the cross hairs against the white ears, and moving side to side, I was able to line up the vertical cross hair between those ears. I fired. After the reverberations of

the shot stilled, all was quiet, and I no longer could see any white or any part of the deer.

Climbing out of my stand, I found a doe, shot in the head. Among the oak trees, it was very dark, and I needed my flashlight to check my watch. It was just 5:25, and the end of the shooting hours. That was a very last minute deer.

Having dressed the deer, I was excited, having seldom stayed in the stand this late, but it had paid off. Reliving the shot, I also thought I saw something run toward the cornfield. Walking in that direction, I found a fawn shot through the chest. That had been my first shot. With my bonus tag, all was legal. I saw how the oak woods could deprive me of half an hour of hunting, so I decided to build a stand at the edge of the woods and the cornfield. This was an eight-foot-high stand. I also built a twelve-foot-high stand along the woods, two hundred yards to the west.

The next year, I spent the first morning in the twelve-foot stand and saw nothing. Moving to my eight-foot stand in the afternoon, I found it to be a better location for watching deer come out in the evening to feed on the corn. With the corn picked, I had a great view over most of the field, over the broken corn stalks and leaves. I could see as far into the corn as I would feel comfortable shooting.

Deer Are Short

By 4:30, with only an hour of shooting time left, I had seen or heard nothing except the usual scurrying of squirrels, that really liked the oak woods, and geese flying overhead, heading south. It got kind of boring looking over the deerless cornfield, so I turned frequently to look back into the woods. With limited visibility in the oaks and the crisp, dry leaves, I expected to hear deer before I saw them. In my boredom, I began to think of my successes of the past and fantasize about where a deer would soon appear. Would it be out of the woods to the left or over the hill. Suddenly something caught my eye, and I studied a strange brown spot in the corn about the size of a football. It quickly disappeared, and I thought it might have been my imagination.

A few seconds later, it appeared again, but in a different location. I realized it was a deer's head. Waiting for it to again lower its head to eat corn, I raised my rifle. The head soon reappeared, again in a different location, but now I was sure it was a deer's head. Taking careful aim, not wanting to cripple the deer with a nose shot, I fired.

As I recovered from the recoil, I saw a deer leaping the corn rows, racing for the safety of the woods about sixty yards to my right. Getting off a shot as it was entering the woods, silence filled in behind the rifle's report. I figured if it had turned left to head down the woods line of trees, I wouldn't have seen it, but if it had gone through the woods into the willow slough, I should have.

As it was getting dark, I waited only ten minutes before going to check it out. With the light failing quickly, I searched for a body or a blood trail. Thirty yards into the wood, I found the deer, a six-point buck lying on the ground facing me. It was hit in the right shoulder and heart. From what I could tell, it had tripped over a deadfall and had gone rack first into the ground, doing a complete somersault.

That night in bed, I relived the day's hunt. I wondered why I didn't see the deer sooner. If it was walking down the row, I should have seen it about 100 yards earlier. I also wondered how I could have missed my first shot. Then the thought popped into my head, *Were there two deer?* I was tempted to get up right then, in the middle of the night, and drive back to the field. I had my bonus tag, so a second deer would be legal.

In this state of quandary, I had trouble getting to sleep, and I awoke before my 4:30 alarm. I got to my stand well before sunrise and planned to stay there watching for deer movement as the sky brightened. But I couldn't keep my eyes off the corn, scrutinizing the spot where I expected my deer was lying if, in fact, there had been two deer, and I had dropped the first. Was it lying in the corn row facing left as I had thought it should be? Was it crumpled up across the corn rows? Was all this my imagination?

As the sun rose above the horizon, I began to get more realistic. I mean, really, could I have dropped two deer in a split second? I was a good hunter but . . . I settled in to watching for deer, enjoying the suspense and excitement of the hunt. Anyway, even if there was a deer lying in the cornfield, it wasn't going anywhere. I decided to enjoy my anticipation another hour before going to check it out. Knowing that twenty minutes would seen like an hour, I checked my watch. When the hour was truly up, I still considered waiting longer.

Finally, I climbed down from the stand and walked the cornfield, crossing each row and looking right and left as if attempting to cross a busy freeway just to make sure I wasn't missing anything. With diminished hopes, I reached the area where I expected the deer to be lying. Going another twenty rows beyond that point, I continued my search. No deer. Okay so no super hunter scenario. I could live with that. Chances were there actually were two deer, a buck following a doe. I had been seeing the doe's head, but at my shot, the timing was that she had just pulled her head back down to eat. I had seen the buck and ignored everything else. The doe could have gone the other way, but, turning to sight on the buck, I never saw her.

As I started back to the stand, another thought crept into my head. Deer really weren't that big. Sure they had long legs, and this gave them the appearance of being rather tall, but they weren't really that large. A two-hundred pound deer was a very large individual. Most were considerably smaller. Most deer stood no more than thirty-two to forty inches at the shoulder. This is nothing close to a half-ton moose or elk. Perhaps this was a lesson in patience and observation. Both of those deer had been almost invisible in a cut-over corn field that was practically flat.

Unbelieveable

The next year, 2009, it was a wet spring for the farmers in Central Minnesota, resulting in the corn being planted late and, subsequently, maturing late. With most of the corn still standing on the deer opener,

I had concerns for the success of the hunt, and also the safety for many hunters. With standing corn, deer might not feel it necessary to leave the fields for the shelter of fence rows and woods. Hunters would know this and many in the area would likely consider walking the fields to drive the deer out. The problem with that was that the risk of other hunters sighting on their buddies increased because the corn hid them. I, too, would be hunting over unpicked corn. I was going to get a hip replacement in two months, and I had limited mobility.

Hunting from my twelve-foot stand, I decided on a method to improve my odds of seeing a deer in the unpicked corn, keeping in mind that the previous year, in the picked-over field, I had trouble seeing deer. I also had picked up a bonus tag at Gander Mountain the day before the season. Standing in the check-out lane of the store, a reporter and photographer from a Minneapolis TV station walked in to interview some hunters on their concerns about the standing corn. As the reporter finished interviewing another hunter, he asked if he could speak to me. So I told him about the plan I had to see better in the corn and maximize my chances of getting a deer. The interviewer seemed interested.

That evening I saw myself on TV describing my plan but none of the others interviewed. Hunting parallel to the corn rows, I needed some way to see into the field and had come up with a new technique. I got permission from my brother-in-law, whose field it was, to bend over the cornstalks just above the ears. This wouldn't interfere with his harvesting. I bent the stalks in the line of the row so it wouldn't interfere with how the deer moved between the rows. I didn't touch the last six rows of the field nearest my stand because I could look down into them well enough without bending over stalks. I hoped this would give the deer a sense of security.

I placed four sight lines in a wagon spoke pattern. If a deer crossed a lane, I hoped I could stop it with a grunt or get it at the next lane. The lanes were four to five feet wide. My center sight line was about eighty yards, straight out from my stand, crossing over the rows. This was my longest line, as it went slightly up hill.

Between my stand and the standing corn was a twenty-foot width of grass and weeds, which was often the deer's travel route. To my right was a twenty-four-inch oak, which was my stand support, but it also blocked my view from deer coming in from my right.

At 8:30 a.m. a doe ran into the sight line from the right and stopped abruptly, looking nervous and excited. It looked back the way it had come, then down my sight line. Then it quickly bounded toward me, leaping over the bent-over corn stalks. After about thirty yards, it made an abrupt right turn in to a corn row before I had a chance to shoot.

By the sound and movements of the corn stalks, it appeared to stop after about twenty feet. Up twelve feet and looking into a slight rise, at forty yards, I couldn't see the deer. I could see a slight shadow area, but not a profile. Knowing it wouldn't stand long, I took a shot at what I assumed would be the chest area.

At the shot, I saw a slight movement from three or four corn stalks, and then quiet. After about ten seconds, I saw a slight movement from another corn stalk, but no indication of a deer moving down the row.

After the shot, I expected one of three things: The doe would run down the corn row, stand still to figure out where the shot came from, or, if hit, drop, struggle and knock down some corn stalks. I envisioned this last option to be a lot more activity than I saw.

I looked at my watch and decided to wait one hour before investigating, watching the area, waiting for movement. Intent on the spot where the doe had been, I wasn't glancing around the tree to check for other deer coming from my right.

About ten minutes later, a fawn came in from my right and raced down the weed area to my left. It would have been a difficult shot as the animal was bounding both vertically and side to side. Chances were I would more likely cripple it than kill it, if I hit it at all. I decided not to shoot.

As I watched the fawn disappear into the corn, a nine-point buck raced by my stand in full pursuit. I got off a shot at about sixty yards, hitting the buck in the spine. It dropped, doing a complete somersault in the process. Looking back, I still saw no movement from the doe.

After waiting ten minutes, I went to dress out the buck. With all the commotion of the second shot and climbing down from my stand, I knew the doe was either dead or just plain gone.

I waited several minutes, fighting suspense. I was enjoying the excitement, not wanting to rush what probably was disappointment. Approaching the area where I thought the deer should be lying, I found nothing. Five more rows, and again, nothing. Another four rows, elation.

The doe lay in a fetal position, between the rows, having disturbed none of the standing corn. It had dropped at the shot, with no struggle. My question—that of all hunters—where had I hit it? I knew it had been running to my left, so I expected to see a wound on the left side. It was lying on its right side, and I saw no entrance wound. I turned the deer over and looked it over head to tail. No wound, but still it was down.

I gutted the deer and found no sign of internal injury. As I raised the deer to drain the body cavity, I noticed a small spot of red hair about an inch below the right eye. (See arrow on photo opposite.) I took a closer look, poked the spot with my finger and discovered it was a bullet hole. Shooting a 30-06, I would have expected the head to be shattered, but it looked pretty much untouched except for the bloody hair.

But the wound was on the right side of the head. The only thing I could figure out was that the doe had to be looking back over her shoulder at the time of the shot, maybe at the buck following the fawn. I made the right choice getting my bonus tag.

This was November 7, 2009, exactly fifty years from the last deer season I had missed. That was November 7, 1959, and I missed it because it was my wedding day.

In 1959, the cost of a deer license was $3.00, and the cost of a marriage license was $5.00.

174

Looking Back

Working in St. Cloud for an engineering firm in the 1960s, near-ly everyone took off the Friday before deer hunting, and we always enjoyed the competing hunting stories after the weekends. One year Dick made a verbal bet on which of us would get the bigger deer. On Monday morning, he rushed into my office, asking if I had gotten a deer. I said I had, a good-sized doe, and, crestfallen, he said he'd gotten a smallish doe or fawn.

Dick went hunting again the next weekend, and again came back on Monday eager to see how I had done. He had gotten a huge buck, and regaled me with all the details about how it had walked out from behind a tree, and how he had dropped it with one shot. A few days later, we were eating lunch, and we were talking about the cost of deer hunting. We talked about spreading out the cost of our clothing, a deer rifle, which usually increased in value over time, and the food we'd been needing for the trip. There was the gas to get to northern Minnesota, the license, buck scent, and other miscellaneous costs. Dick figured his total cost for that year's hunting at $7.50. In questioning the low amount, he said that selling the hide paid for the license and his party had shared the gas. I still thought this was really low, but he wouldn't shake on his $7.50, so I asked him if he had included the cost of his shells. He said, "I only took two shots, and one of them was at a target."

After a brief hesitation, I asked, "You shot two deer on different weekends . . . did you use the same bullet over again?"

Dick got red in the face, and one of his hunting buddies, Paul, turned, got up, and walked out of the room, holding back a laugh. He knew Dick had been given a deer the first weekend from one of the hunters who stayed up for the week.

In Retrospect

Having to learn my deer hunting by trial and error, I think my experiences were more memorable. If I had been mentored by other hunters and followed their advice, I likely wouldn't have written this book, not having had a wealth of experiences, both good and bad. Hunters with much more experience than mine will be reading this book, but here are some suggestions I believe will improve the success of less-experienced hunters.

When taking a person hunting for the first time, take him to a stand with a view over a large area, giving him a greater chance to see deer and other wildlife. You want to keep them interested.

Always wear a cap with a brim. I have missed shots at deer because of the sun in my eyes, and a cap minimized that risk. One time I tried to hold a hand over my eyes and shoot one handed. I missed that deer.

If walking in brush, especially in the dark, wear eye protection. It cost me a deer, one standing broadside to me at thirty yards, because a branch had hit me in the eye, and my eyes watered too much to be able to sight.

A comfortable stand, preferably on a swivel, with a back rest set at the height for comfortable shooting can really extend those long hours of sitting and waiting.

I was raised on a farm where I was accustomed to animals and would remain relatively calm at the sight of deer. That's something that's particularly hard for some people. I take care on my first shot, as it is often the only one I'll get, and is usually my best opportunity to harvest a deer. But being over-excited compromises that. Inexperienced hunters tend to fumble their first shot at deer by being excited and not thinking through what should be done to succeed. That takes practice.

When shooting at a deer that runs off and disappears, many hunters assume they missed it. Not necessarily. Check for blood at the location of the possible hit, and at the place where you thought it disappeared. If in doubt, ask for the assistance of an experienced hunter.

I always like two or more stands, for several reasons. One is that the wind may affect which is the better one on a given day, sometimes by the direction of the wind. If I get bored, I can improve my attention and expectations by changing stands.

If in a hilly area, I will place one stand on higher ground, and one on lower. In the morning, as the temperature rises, the air currents will rise, along with my scent. Using a stand on higher ground keeps me hidden longer. In the evening, when it cools, scents travel downhill. A lower stand, then, is a better choice.

As an experienced hunter, I can often tell where a deer was hit by how it reacted to the shot. The color of the blood can also be a clue. Where the blood is found on the trail is important. Is it in the tracks or maybe rubbed off against brush as the deer passes.

Many of us have fallen off or out of a stand, but most of us are too embarrassed to tell anyone about it. And, yes, it happened to me. I had a stand nine feet off the ground with two-by-fours nailed to a tree as steps. I arrived at my stand well before sun up and threw my lunch up into the stand and then proceeded to carry up my rifle. I had one hand on the rifle and one on the steps. I was five feet off the ground and

Converting Beef into Venison

It's possible to convert farm-raised beef into a product that tastes like venison, but it requires both dedication and effort. For those who love venison and want to get that "wild" taste, though, it's well worth it.

1. When choosing your calf, look for the "runt" of the herd.
2. Feed the calf weeds, slough grass, tree buds, twigs, and acorns.
3. Before butchering, turn the calf loose in a strange woods and chase it around for at least a couple of hours to get the blood and adrenalin into the meat.
4. Have a hunting experience. Use your shotgun, making sure to get at least one slug into each hind quarter. This adds fur and fiber.
5. Take your 4-wheeler and drag the calf through the woods and at least one cattail slough. This adds additional fiber.
6. Haul the animal home on the hood or fender of your vehicle to add that "road flavor" and start some curing.
7. Hang the calf in the garage for a week. This gets the attention of the neighbors and adds that carbon monoxide flavor
8. When you see the neck stretching, it's time to cut up your "venison."

You may never go back to beef!

placed my rifle over the edge of the stand. But then I lost my grip. As I began to fall, I was able to finish pushing my rifle onto the platform.

I fell flat on my back and was temporarily knocked out. When I came to, my first instinct was to rush up into my stand. Not a good idea. Not when your mind was in a fog.

Getting into the stand, I saw somebody's lunch on the floor. I immediately thought that someone else was using my stand. My mind went sort of balistic until I realized it was my own lunch, one I had thrown up earlier.

Getting down at noon, I checked where I had fallen. Some brush had been around my stand, and I had sawn off the stems about four inches above the ground. Most of those sawed-off stumps were from half an inch to an inch in diameter. I somehow had been lucky enough not to land on any of them. How my body landed between some of them was amazing as they protruded from the ground on either side of where I had landed. I was lucky I hadn't punctured a lung.

A final tip when hunting with youngsters: "BRING FOOD!"

Good Hunting!

Part Four

Fishing

20

Fishing by Accident

MY FIRST FISHING EXPERIENCES came more by accident than by purpose.

The first summer, my grandparents took me to a friend's cabin at Lake Florida, but not with any intention of fishing. Having no one to play with, I saw a wooden boat on shore and wanted to go fishing. Eventually someone found an old rod and a reel, a bobber, and some old rusty hooks. I dug worms from one of the gardens. My grandfather rowed to an area of weeds and cattails, baited my hook for me and watched as I fished.

After half an hour I had only caught a tiny bass, but I was excited. It was my first fish! But then Granddad told me I had to throw it back. Not only was it small but bass season wasn't opened yet. I didn't want to. I just couldn't throw back my first fish. I wanted to take it home and show Mother.

My grandparents finally agreed. They put it into a one-pound butter carton to sneak it home.

The next year my grandparents took me out to their cabin again, along with my young cousin. My cousin and I were playing outside while my grandparents were in the cabin. I was supposed to be keeping an eye on her. We were watching some boys cannonballing off the dock into the water, when she walked out onto the dock and simply jumped off the end. The water was well over her head, so that all that remained near the surface were her long, dark, wavy curls.

I reached down into the water off the end of the dock and grabbed those curls. With a few bounces, I managed to get her back onto the dock. She was wet and sputtering, but she was okay.

I have very good recall of past events, and that memory, some fifty years after the event, was still strong. But, had I somehow imagined my rescue? I asked her parents, and they didn't remember. So I asked my cousin if she recalled falling off the dock when she was young. She looked at me and immediately replied, "No, I didn't fall off the dock. I jumped. I saw those boys jumping off, and it looked like fun. I decided I wanted to have fun like that too. So I jumped off."

She also remembered that she was four and I was seven at the time. She didn't recall how I managed to pull her out, though. Probably for the best.

I did no further fishing until we were on the farm and some of Herman's relatives came up from Iowa and wanted to go fishing. Herman had only one ancient rod and reel, one I had never seen him use, but the Iowa relatives had an extra one I could use. Excited, I dug some worms, and we headed to Lake Andrew to rent a boat. We discovered, however, that the boat only had seats for three people. I was the fourth. I was left on shore with the borrowed rod and reel, set up with a bobber and hook, and a few worms. They suggested I fished off shore.

The rig was an old level-wind reel, and I had never cast any type of rod and reel. I had quite a time. Not knowing how to thumb the line, I was getting constant back lashes and was smacking my bobber in the water or on the ground. Another fisherman was watching me, and finally took pity on me and came over. He showed me how to cast, and told me there was a better place to fish.

Down the road a short distance, a small creek went beneath the road, through some woods, and emptied into the lake. As it was spring and the water was high, much of the woods was flooded with up to two feet of water. I could wade out into the woods and could actually see the fish that had come "inland" to eat. I saw sunfish and bass. In the flowing water, I could let my bobber drift, so I didn't have to cast. But with my oversized bobber and hook, I only caught two tiny sunfish, but they were big to me.

As I was about to go back to meet Herman and the Iowans, some other fishermen gave me three eating-sized sunfish.

When the boat returned, Herman and the other had not caught a single fish. I proudly showed them my five. I didn't have much sympathy for them because they had left me behind, and I didn't tell them I had been given the three big ones.

Another time, a friend came down from Minneapolis to take Herman and me fishing at Nest Lake. We were going to troll for northerns, but it was a row boat, so one person had to be rowing and not fishing. It was mid-summer and very windy, and we were constantly dragging in the weeds. I had one especially large bunch that attached to my

185

hook, and was just reeling it in to clean it off yet again when that bunch of weeds started to fight. When I pulled the line in, I indeed had a large clump of weeds on the hook as well as a five-pound northern. It was the only fish the group of us caught that day. That night, when Herman's friend was about to leave, he offered me five dollars for the fish. That was a lot of money in the 1940s. I don't know if he was serious or not, but I wasn't about to part with my fish.

Fishing the Dam

My parents would go to Willmar each Saturday to buy groceries and would drop me off to fish by the dam at the west end of Willmar Lake. Water only flowed over the dam in early spring and maybe for a short time after a heavy rain, limiting my opportunities. When it flowed over the dam, the water dropped into an area of large rocks and then down a small creek. In the spring some small fish, mostly bullheads, would swim up the creek and would hide in the pools near the rocks below the dam. The water seldom measured more than eighteen inches deep.

I would walk or crawl across the rocks, reaching down in the watery crevasses for fish. I quickly learned about the sharp and painful spines the bullhead sported on its dorsal and pectoral fins.

I never caught many fish at the dam, maybe six to eight small bullheads each time. They were always small, I was proud of them and took them home to eat. My family wasn't big on fish, but they insisted that, if I caught them, I should eat them. No problem for me. I liked the flavor of bullheads. Herman taught me how to clean them while avoiding the spines and how to skin them, using a hammer, a nail, a knife, and a pair of pliers.

One day I caught something a little different from the usual bullheads. I grabbed it, and it felt like a broom handle with rough scales, but it sure wriggled. The fish was about eighteen inches long—huge compared to five- and six-inch bullheads—and was shaped like a broom stick with a mouth like a needle-nosed pliers. Frankly, the fish scared me to death. I quickly threw it back and scrambled out of there.

Herman didn't know what it could be, so I looked it up in the library. It was a gar. I later caught a second one, thought I was pretty sure it was the same one again. I have never seen one since.

Having Herman's old rod and reel and learning how to cast, I began walking to two small nearby lakes, George and Henderson, about four miles away. I would fish off shore. I only caught small sunfish and small bass, but it was enjoyable.

When I was seventeen and a senior in high school, a dam burst on the west side of Lake Florida, and a large number of fish escaped into the slough. With the slough as large as the lake, suddenly the fish had a large area to roam. I believe the part of the slough by our farm was the deepest part of the new system, and seemed to attract the greatest number of fish.

Spring-fed creeks flowed into the slough near our farm, and they also seemed to attract northerns. The great part was that I could see them from the shore. I would wade into the three feet of water, about fifteen feet from shore and cast, using a frog as bait. Many northerns would follow the frog, but few would bite. The water was so clear, I could watch them follow my bait as I led them around between me and the shore.

During the heat of summer, fishing slowed down, but it picked up again in the fall. Before going to school in the moring, I would cast a few times from shore, often getting my three-fish limit. I once caught three fish in four casts.

That fall we had a heavy snow after the ice had formed, which can make it difficult for fish survival by reducing the oxygen in the water. One of the spring-fed creeks kept a small area of water near the shore open, and it soon began to get larger. Hundreds of minnows were coming in, apparently short on oxygen, and their combined movement eroded the ice. Within two weeks, the opening grew to eight feet across and the mass of minnows seemed almost solid.

As the water was only about twelve inches deep, I soon began to see the dorsal fins of northerns through the writhing minnows. They never came during the day, but only at night, and well after sunset at that. I'd go down with a flashlight to watch them. I'd shine my light directly on them. They were to be entirely covered in minnows except for those protruding dorsal fins. By carefully wading through the minnows, I could grab the northerns and toss them up onto the shore. I usually would get only one or two before the rest spooked. Then the water seemed to boil with the panicked fish as they all tried to get to the safety of the ice-covered water. I would often wait about two hours and go back, and there would often be more northerns among the minnows.

I found an old rusty fishing spear somewhere and fitted it with an eight-foot tree-branch handle. Holding it parallel to the ice, I would push it under the edge of the ice. Often I would get two northerns at a time because they were so crowded. They were small ones, usually only one to one and one-half pounds, but I was only pushing the spear, not throwing it. I once had four on the spear at once. But after one thrust, fishing would be done for the night.

After a week, I could tell the fish were getting more sluggish, and there were even more numerous, if that were possible. They were less disturbed by my fishing activities, too. Then they started filling the open space during the daylight hours as well as at night. One day I caught thirty-three northerns, but that was the last day of any numbers. Clearly the fish were running out of oxygen. I began to bring up dead fish while spearing. My spearing got me a few larger fish now, up to two pounds.

The open water had increased in size by the activity of the fish and grown to about twelve feet across, but with the increase of dead fish, I stopped spearing.

The next spring, our shore was lined with dead fish, in some areas solidly out to about ten feet. These were mostly carp and northerns, but I saw many small sunfish and crappies. The largest carp I saw was over six pounds, and the largest northern was about five pounds. Most of the dead fish were along our shore on the southeast side of the

slough, the fish being blown in by the northwest winds. Of course, because of the open water and the springs, many of those fish might have been on this side of the slough anyway.

Some fish did survive, but not enough to make fishing in the slough worthwhile that summer. The next winter I was in Minneapolis for school, but I discovered that the Minnesota Department of Natural Resources was trying to save some of the remaining fish in the slough as they were again short of oxygen and coming into our springs. One Friday they constructed a wooden trough/flume on shore and set up a gas-powered water pump. The flume was about eight feet high and they were pumping water to the top of it and letting it flow onto the ice, opening a large area, hoping it would attract the fish and allow them to attract a larger number of fish. They then planned to net fish out to take to a lake with better oxygen. After two day, though, they had no success and decided to wait until the heavy run came into our springs. Checking the springs every day, they chose a night when I was at school to net them. They had a water tanker ready to transport the rescued fish and a large crew to net them. They worked through the night. I later heard they had saved about 2,200 northerns, and they put the fish back into Lake Florida.

The next weekend when I was home, I discovered that many smaller fish—crappie, sunfish, and bullheads—lay in the ice around the spring, but without all the larger fish to keep the hole open, the ice had claimed most of the open water. Come spring there were some dead fish on our shore but nothing like the numbers from the year before. Many of the small bullheads did survive, and my younger sister would fish for them off shore.

After my folks moved, I knew there were years when many of the fish would survive over winter providing good fishing in the summer, and then other years when large winter kills claimed a heavy toll. I was back at the farm a few years ago just after the ice went out, and there were again a large number of dead fish on shore.

190

Small bullheads.

Living in Minneapolis, with school and working, I had few opportunities to fish, but Wayne and I did locate a rather secluded lake in North Central Minnesota as my deer stories indicated. There were three deer camps or summer cabins on the lake, but we seldom saw another boat. It was a long, narrow lake with woods and hills on all sides, making it deep and fishable in any weather.

It was always a sure thing that we would get small northerns, along with a few panfish. I did catch one walleye, a five-pounder, but it was the beauty of the area that was the real attraction. By one of the hunting cabins was a small dock and on the shore was a small building, some ten feet by ten feet. It was badly deteriorated, but it often served as our "cabin" if it wasn't raining. We would pile a bunch of grass or pine boughs for a mattress, lay a large, heavy blanket below us, then put our sleeping bags on top of that, making a bed for the four of us. There was always a bit of fight for space.

We fished in two boats, and I hooked the biggest fish I had ever experienced on that lake. I had heavy, braided line, but when I pulled up,

191

it just pulled back down. I thought it was snagged. We were in only six feet of water, so we called over the other boat to help get off the snag. Getting to where the fish was snagged, they began to laugh. I had hooked the end of a pine tree that had been in the water many years, but it still had plenty of spring in the tip.

After a snapping turtle had its fill.

After we had gone in, leaving our fish tied to the dock, we went to select fish for our breakfast. But when we pulled up the stringer, we discovered only the skeletons of our catch. We had been visited by a snapping turtle.

Jim, who lived near the lake, told us of several other remote lakes in the area. Our favorite is now a small public camp ground, McCarty Lake. It now has an improved gravel road, but years ago, that was only a trail through the woods. At that time, the lake was off the main trail and somewhat hidden among the trees. Others knew of the lake and had hidden a wooden row boat and oars on the shore. We never saw the owner, but on several occasions we borrowed the boat. All we caught were northerns, but we saw evidence that there were crappies in the lake as well. Traveling along the shore, we found a great spot to bobber fish near a small point. It was a sure thing for northerns, and the fish grew bigger here than on our other lake.

As a trail was improved along the lake, it became more popular with fishermen and campers, and, predictably, our success fishing diminished as well.

Years Later

SOME YEARS LATER, WHEN LOWELL WAS SEVEN, we took a chance and fished the lake. We had limited success with the fish, but great with the wildlife. Coming around the point, we surprised two busy beavers, and they mostly ignored us. Lowell found a beautiful souvenier, a four-foot piece of popple, autographed on each end by the beavers. It had their teeth marks on it where they had chewed off the bark.

Just a short distance beyond the beavers, we heard an angry snort and then stomping feet. Apparently we had disturbed a doe with her fawn. Heading back along the shore, we saw a mink with a red squirrel in its jaws. It was racing through the woods and into some tall grass. Soon there was rustling in the grass. It was apparently feeding its young. We really didn't care that the fishing was poor that day.

One winter I took our family to McCarty Lake to try ice fishing and get a view of the beauty of the woods in the dead of winter. It was not yet the time for tip-up fishing gear, and we just had wooden sticks with a spike on one end to jab into the ice to support the line. Fishing was poor, but Lowell found some other excitement. As we jabbed the spike end of our fishing sticks into the the ice, we would hear a rumble as the ice cracked entending out across the lake.

It was a very cold day, and with the temperature rapidly dropping further, it was causing the ice to contract. As it did so, it would develop its own cracks, causing other rumbles across the lake. But jabbing the spike into the ice would offer instant relief for the contracting ice, and it cracked and rumbled instantly.

Lowell walked around the lake, causing about fifteen rumbles, and he watched as some extended all the way across the lake, though others ended when they hit existing cracks. After he had used up all the rumbles, he got out his hockey stick and a puck. As there were large areas of clear ice, he had fun knocking around the puck. However, there were also some impressive snow drifts. Just before we had to leave, he hit the puck hard, and it buried itself in one of those drifts. He searched but we had to leave, and he had to leave it. So, there is a hockey puck in McCarty Lake that I doubt anyone will ever find again. Not a great loss.

When we fished, we played the game of guessing the weight of the fish we caught. We'd weigh them when we got home. We got pretty good at estimating weights. We came to shore one time to find a fisherman holding up a four-pound northern and telling his friends it was seven or eight pounds. Lowell looked at me and smiled.

When we moved to St. Cloud, we had closer access to many lakes. Our first rental apartment was on the Mississippi River. I joined the Jaycees and made many fishermen friends, and Mille Lacs became a favorite lake.

Stubborn

One fishing opener, four of us went up to Mille Lacs, planning to stay overnight. With our confidence in the fishing, we didn't get on the lake until 1:00, with the best fishing beginning about 9:00 p.m. With two to a boat, we planned to meet on shore at 6:00 to plan our evening fishing and check on bragging rights. I had caught six walleyes and my boat partner one. The other boat had one and one. My friend in the other boat was strict about using a spinner-and-minnow configuration. I had a green jig and a minnow. Back at shore about 11:00, I had caught an additional three walleye, and he had one more.

The next morning I had three walleye in the first half hour. My partner said, "He's watching you," referring to my friend in the next boat. That boat soon disappeared, and I assumed those guys had gone to a new location on the lake. Meeting in the afternoon to go home, those guys said they had hauled out and gone to Farm Island Lake, north of Mille Lacs, but they had similar luck, catching only one fish. I was now up to seventeen.

My friend and I went up one evening the next weekend, each of us using our favorite bait. I caught four fish, and he netted one. By the next trip he had switched to a jig and minnow.

Kid's Luck

WHEN LOWELL WAS NINE, WE WENT fishing northerns at Mille Lac, with two of Lowell's friends and their dad in their boat. We were among fifteen other boats in the bay. Not wanting to lose our large minnows on a backlash, I cast for Lowell. As the northerns would often circle, leaving much slack line in the water, I would take in the slack line and pass the rod to Lowell, telling him when to set the hook.

We began fishing at 9:00. By 3:00, Lowell had seven northerns all from five and one-half to eleven pounds. I had none. His friends had

only one. By mid-afternoon they decided to go home. Lowell and I planned to stay overnight in the back of our pickup, so I asked his friends' dad if he would take our fish back. They headed to shore and tossed our fish in their boat for the trip home.

We caught two more small northerns in the morning, but we had little action around us in other boats. Guys in a nearby boat were talking about the poor luck when one said, "Yesterday a kid caught seven."

Lowell looked at me and quickly said, "Do you think he was talking about me?"

We had no camera on the lake and were anxious to get home to get a picture of Lowell with his big fish. When we arrived home, my wife said, "You're not going to like it. Look in the freezer."

We found seven dried, shriveled northerns that had been gutted. Lowell's friends had left the fish in an uncovered aluminum boat in the bright sun for the one-and-one-half-hour drive back to St. Cloud. After putting the fish in our freezer, they went home but thought better of it and came back to gut the fish. As his wife was friends with mine, she came too and told her, "Isn't Bob lucky to have a friend like my husband?"

Take a Friend

I GOT TO KNOW AN OLDER FARMER in a small neighboring town who had broken his back in a tractor accident and had lost the use of his legs. He had also recently lost his wife, but he still resided on the farm, renting out the land. I would take him fishing each summer, and he enjoyed it. He had to walk with crutches and sit on a small inner tube, but he always seemed in good spirits.

On one trip to Mille Lacs, I caught a twelve-pound northern. Despite his lack of mobility, he enjoyed netting it. A little later, I hooked a twelve-pound mate to the first. A nearby boat, having seen his strug-

Lowell and Lynae.

gle landing the first fish came over with their big net to assist. We really didn't need the help, but they meant well. I kept trying to guide the northern to my friend's net, as we had two nets splashing in the water. And I was able to give him a thrill, thought not without some fears of losing the fish.

Another time we were fishing in a launch, and I caught an eight-pound walleye. There were four in our group, and I offered to give the fish to them but using a numbers game. With luck, my disabled friend won. Sitting in his wheelchair, I stood a foot away and told him to hold out his hands as I tossed the fish. I said, "Now you can truthfully say you caught it." I met his son a few weeks later, and he thanked me for taking his dad fishing and said, "That was sure a big fish dad caught, wasn't it?"

The dad was also a well-liked mayor in his small town, and, hearing of his great catch, his constituents bowed to him.

On one trip, he told me the person farming his land had cheated him out of a year's corn crop. He always seemed cheerful, and it wasn't until a few years later that I realized how much he was hiding.

For a full mount, I was waiting for a big fish to mount, but a twelve-pounder wasn't big enough. These were my two biggest fish to date, though, so I decided to have their heads mounted on a three-leaf clover-shaped board, leaving the third leaf for a larger fish. I went to a local taxidermist, Gene Bzdok, and told thim I needed a fish at least three pounds bigger for the bottom leaf. He just smiled.

Big Surprise

THE NEXT YEAR, I INVITED TWO NEIGHBORS, Dick and Bob, to fish the opener with me. I showed them my cloverleaf. One said, "If a fish that large is in our boat, I'm leaving."

We planned to fish walleyes at dusk and stay overnight in a camper, so we were in no hurry to fish early. Getting to the bay at 9:30, there were about fifteen boats out, but little action. We decided we would fish walleyes first in another area of the lake and check back later to see if the action had picked up. It proved to be a good choice. By 4:00 we had half our limit of eighteen walleye. I decided to check the bay. Now there were fewer boats—several had apparently either moved or given up—and the action had not improved. But two ten-pound northerns had been caught. They were tied to boats back on the shore. I suggested we try to fill our limits of walleys, which we did, and fish for northerns the next morning. Seeing the two ten-pounders gave me confidence.

Only half the numbers of boats returned to the lake the next morning but none were on my favorite spot for northerns. As it was a large bay with little variation in depth, I had located some productive locations. I had explained my fishing method to my buddies the previous day. It went like this: To reduce the resistance on the line when a fish took the bait, I liked a submarine-shaped bobber that was weighted so that little of it showed on the surface. It would often allow a large minnow to bounce it below the surface, which often was the sign that a northern was approaching. I left the drag off, and when a fish hit, I gave it free line until it stopped. Northerns would often grab a minnow and run. They then would stop so it could be turned and swallowed. Then they'd take off again. When the northern first stopped, the bobber would pop up, and I would take up any slack in the line. When the fish took off again, I'd give it about ten feet and then solidly set the hook.

We were fishing in about seven feet of water, with Bob in the front of the boat, Dick in the middle, and me at the motor. After half an hour, Bob yelled, raised his rod and set the hook. He hadn't waited, however, and reeled back only a scarred up minnow. A short time later, Dick's bobber started acting up. He was fishing to the right of the boat and about twenty feet from the motor. The bobber would go down for a few seconds, pop up, then go down again. It was slowly making a twelve-inch circle. It was too much action for the minnow alone and not typical of a northern. I thought it might be a large bullhead, as there were some one-pounders in the bay. They were still too small to swallow the large minnows used for northern fishing, but they did like to mouth them. After watching these little "bobs" for a while, I told Dick to point the rod toward the bobber, and when I said, "Now!" give it a hard set. He did, but he said, "I got something on the line, but it's not a bullhead."

The fish swam toward the motor, keeping near the bottom. With a serious bend to Dick's rod. As it was heading directly for the motor and I didn't want it to foul, I reached out with the palm of my hand to guide the line around the prop. As I touched the line, the fish either felt me or saw me, and it exploded. I had to make it quick to get the line around the motor, not knowing that Dick's rod was now over my shoulder. Inadvertently, I looped the line over the rod tip, and the line summarily snapped. Based on the pressure on the line, I told Dick it had to have been at least a seven- or eight-pounder. We were now zero for two.

I had just started to rig up Dick's line when Bob yelled, "There's a bobber." Sure enough, about fifteen feet in front of our boat, Dick's bobber had surfaced. It was moving slowly with about six feet of line trailing behind. I quickly pulled in my line and told Bob to pull in his and pull up the anchor, as we were in for a chase.

Starting the motor, we slowly headed for the bobber, but, as we neared it, it disappeared, but we could still see it just below the surface as the fish raced away. Losing sight of the bobber, I slowed the boat, and it surfaced again about thirty feet away. As we approached it again, the fish would race away, the bobber would submerge and we had to slow. Then it would pop up again.

I had placed the hook about thirty inches off the bottom, and, assuming the fish would rest as close to the bottom as possible, we really shouldn't have seen the bobber at all. I believed there was just enough bouyancy in the bobber to cause a little irritation to the fish's jaw, and it rose in the water to relieve it.

As I neared the still bobber, I shut off the motor, wanting to glide in, but the boat always seemed to stop short of it. I told Bob to hang over the edge of the boat and wrap the trailing line around his hand, but not to touch the bobber. After several tries, Bob was able to take hold of the line and wrap it around his hand, but he then attempted to pull on it, and the line began to cut into his hand. He then knew this was even bigger than an eight-pounder. We finally managed to pull the fish into the boat, and what we had was a fourteen-pounder.

With the fish in the boat, I rushed back to my favorite spot. But I noticed I couldn't get much speed going. The anchor was dragging.

Back at our spot, we found that, in our haste, we had also forgotten to pull in our minnow pail. Out of the remaining fifteen minnows, only three were alive, and those were sluggish. Baiting up, I hoped it was my turn, and it was. It didn't take long before I had hooked and landed a fifteen-pounder and it was even before we had gotten the first fish on the stringer.

Heading to shore after that, I told my buddies to put the fish on the rope stringer while I went for more bait. When I got back, the fish were in the water, one lying on its side and both missing a few scales. It hadn't occurred to me that they didn't know how to string a northern. They had put the fish on shore, limited their mobility with their knees on either side of the fish's head and forced the metal tip of the stringer through the bones on the upper and lower jaws.

We fished two more hours, but the excitement was over.

The next morning, I was back at the taxidermist with my fifteen-pound, four-ounce northern for the bottom leaf. I told him if I caught anything larger, a fish over eighteen pounds, I would mount the entire fish. Gene again smiled.

The next year, on opener, it happened, an eighteen-pound, five-ounce northern. But that was my last year of big fish until a twenty-one-pound, fourteen-ounce northern in 1986, fourteen years later. That fish was weighed in at Bitzens Bait on Mille Lacs, and a picture was taken for their local paper. It was the largest northern reported in the state on opening weekend that year.

Lay Flat?

I HAD OFTEN HEARD THAT, WHEN HOOKING a large northern, the fish would often lie on the bottom, resisting efforts to reel it in. Stan and I may have proven that wrong.

We were bobber fishing in about seven feet of water when Stan hooked a good-sized fish. After a few strong passes, it came toward the boat and stopped directly below Stan's rod tip. It had its nose in the mud and the body vertical, parallel to the line. Only its large, reddish tail was visible in the water. It slowly moved from side to side to help keep up the pressure.

And Stan was all for putting pressure on the fish, but I said to just hold it tight. After a few minutes, the fish moved out of the mud, fought for a few minutes, then headed back down, head-first in the mud. It slowly tired and Stan pulled in a ten-pounder. A short time later, I landed a twelve-pounder, which acted the same. It was curious and beautiful to watch the fish dance upside down in the water.

Above, left: Bob with a twenty-one-pounder. Top, right: An eighteen-pounder. Bottom, right: Bob, Bob, and Dick.

Ice piled on Mille Lacs and ice on shore. A week later I got my eighteen-pounder.

Need Patience

MY FATHER-IN-LAW, KEN, WAS ALWAYS BUSY on the farm, but with a son to do the milking, I finally pursuaded him to go fishing with me on Mille Lacs some evenings. I don't think he had fished in forty years and was reluctant to go, but after I talked him into it, he seemed game.

I picked up Ken at 6:30 p.m. and we drove up to Mille Lacs. He was doubtful that we could catch any fish, and maybe, had he been anyone else, I might have agreed with him. We parked along the bay and then took the mile ride to the island. We would be trowling in three to five feet of water along the shore. We had a fish or two by 8:30, sunset, but then caught our limit of twelve by 10:30. Ken enjoyed the outing and wanted to go back.

We did the next week. It was a cloudy, dark night, but that was good weather for fishing. We used floating rappalas with a lead sinker

and monofilament line. Fishing in the dark, however, has its risks. We were making a corner around the island, and managed to get our lines badly tangled. I thought it best to cut one of the lines, so I pulled Ken's lure into the boat. In the poor light, I cut the line on my lure, which was still over the side of the boat. It promptly sank out of sight. Rigging up again, we again caught our limit. Now Ken was hooked.

The next week, we were trolling in the same area when I got a light snag. Reeling in, I saw I had snagged the rappala from the week before. The sinker had held the floating line below the water's surface, and the lure hung above the sinker by twelve inches. We again filled out, and I enjoyed the evening fishing. In fact, though I typically get more enjoyment being with someone, but those evening fishing sessions were so much fun, I'd go alone if I had to. I often enjoy the peace and quiet of fishing alone, and the evening easily provided that, as well as some-times amazing sunsets over the lake.

Close Call

THAT EVENING, A STORM WAS COMING IN. Impending storms usually improved fishing, and when I reached the island, several other boats were there, fishing in deeper water than I generally fished. The larger boats would have a difficult time in the shallow water and were con-stantly turning. Trolling by the southeast side of the island, I was having some luck, but I was waiting for "the good bite" as it got dark.

Because of the coming storm, it got dark earlier than normal, and, along with my luck, the wind picked up. The lights of the other boats gradually disappeared as they headed for the various resorts. When they came out for night fishing, they usually stayed until midnight. But it was getting windy, and I was having some trouble controlling the boat. But the fish were biting and that was my main focus. I soon real-ized that the lights of the last boat were getting smaller as the boat head-ed for its dock.

I was still a fish short of my limit, but with the wind still picking up and knowing that my five-and-a-half-horsepower motor was going to have to struggle to get me back to shore. I didn't really want to be on the lake alone on such a night. As I curled around the southeast corner of the island, the sheltered side, I figured out quickly why they had all left as I encountered four-foot waves. Mille Lacs is a shallow lake, big but not very deep. As such, when the wind started pushing the water, it quickly made significant waves.

I had to go west to get back to shore, facing a strong northwest wind. This immediately caused problems. Trying to go west, the wind would catch the front of the boat and attempt to throw me back into the trough between the waves. If I was caught by waves, the boat could easily capsize. I had to drive directly into the waves, burst over the crest, making a sharp turn to the left down the backside of the wave, but be ready to face the next wave head on.

Gaining the crest was difficult. With the bow in the air, catching the wind, my small motor was fighting both the waves and the wind. I had to gain height to get to each wave's crest, but I was slowly being pushed backwards by the wind and gravity. After I finally gained a crest, with the bow of the boat high in the air, I would drop over like a teeter-totter. I would speed down the backside of a wave, gaining both speed and distance, and then fight the next wave.

As I came around the island, I had heard wailing sirens, but I had ignored them as I had more serious problems. As the sirens continued, it finally connected that this was a warning to get off the lake. I agreed with that.

I saw a light shining along the west shore. It became my beacon, my destination, but in the darkness I couldn't tell if I was making any progress toward it.

I don't believe I was ever really scared, mostly because I had to concentrate so tightly on controlling the boat and coaxing the motor. Every wave had to be conquered with precision or I risked capsizing. I fought up each crest, fought my way down, all the while trying to gain

207

as much distance towards the west as I could. The motor would rev up when I went down the backside of waves, then struggle hard going up each new one. As the boat flopped over the crest of a wave, the motor would come entirely out of the water for a few seconds and rev up.

Finally, I could see slow progress. My beacon was slowly growing stronger, brighter. Then I began to feel the benefit of the tall rushes from the bay breaking the wind and lowering the height of the waves. I passed the rushes and entered the bay, and I knew the crisis was over. My body finally relaxed, and only then did I realize how tense it had been. It was a beautiful feeling coming into the calmer water, and even more amazing joy when I felt the bottom of the boat grind over gravel. Safe now, I sat in the boat several minutes, too limp to get up and out of the boat.

I looked at my watch. Eleven. I had left the island about 9:30. For an hour and a half, I had fought my way across that part of the lake in dangerous water.

As I loaded the boat and then left the bay, the sirens still wailed. I felt fortunate to be on my way home safely after that ordeal. Putting the boat away the next morning, I noticed that there was only a light slush in my fuel tank. I lifted it, then checked. I had less than half a gallon of fuel left. I believe the sharp angle of the boat had kept the fuel over the suction hose. If I had run out of fuel, I would have been in very dire straites as the east shore of the lake at that point was twelve miles away. I doubt I would have made it without the motor helping stay angled properly to the waves.

21

Ice Fishing

New Experience

To MANY, WINTER IN MINNESOTA IS A TIME to head south or sit by a warm fire. To me it is a a time of greatest enjoyment in fishing. This is partly due to a lack of other outdoor activities and maybe being Scandinavian. It might not sound like fun to someone else, but I relished the hours of solitude I faced staring down into a hole in the ice, watching for that "twitch" of my bobber.

I was fishing in the bay on Mille Lac when an Indian from the nearby reservation came out to fish. It looked like he had a twelve-inch length of broom handle for a bobber. It had gouges cut out of all sides and was painted in bright earth colors. With his fishing line wrapped around the handle, he bridged his hole with the stick and lowered his hook and bait. When a fish hit, it would spin the stick, making a rumbling sound on the edge of the ice hole. I was fascinated. He called this his "rumble stick." Getting a bite, he would hold the stick in both hands, using his grip as a drag. Then he would slowly roll the line up around the stick. I only saw him once and I wish I had offered to buy his rumble stick as it was so unusual.

I enjoyed fishing for northerns with tip-ups, and I was allowed two lines on the ice. I also enjoyed fishing with my grandsons. Any "flag

up" was exciting for everybody, and, as we took turns with the tip-ups, there was always the questions, "Who's turn is it?"

When ice fishing, I have a small collapsible fish house that I normally transport with me, rather than invest in a larger, more solid fishhouse that would remain on the lake all winter. It was also used more to carry my supplies than as a shelter. I enjoyed hole hopping and the ability to move around the lake when the fish were biting in another location. Fish move around, and I enjoyed trying to keep up with them.

Seems Odd

ONE DAY I NOTICED A FISH HOUSE with the name of a seldom-seen friend on it. Going over, I was greeted and invited in to discover he had a hole in the ice about two feet wide. We were fishing sunfish, so I wondered why such a large hole. I mean, a hole that size might be opened in the shallows where people spear northerns, but to fish sunnies? I was confused.

A few weeks later, I heard the reason when he was visited by the game warden. A taxidermist had alerted the warden after he had been asked to mount a large musky with large hook wounds under its jaw. The fish looked like it had been snagged. As the lake was well-known for its muskies, I had seen many while "sight fishing" for sunfish. One day I had muskies go below my hole nine times. The big predatory fish would often lie beneath the hole, possibly attracted by the open hole or the shadow of the fish house.

Some of the most interesting ice fishing is in the spring before the ice goes out. Then I fish in four feet of water. The tops of the rushes of course had long since frozen into the ice, but, as the snow melts and creeks and rivers flow into the lake, the ice began to float with the higher water level, and the rushes could be pulled up by the roots, exposing thousands of bugs and larvae that had wintered in the mud. This became a fish smorgasbord, attracting a lot of fish.

Sitting in my collapsible house, it was like watching an aquarium. The insects and small crustations were food mainly for the panfish, but those fish were the food source for larger fish. I could often seen several fish in my hole at one time, and, interestingly, the smaller ones were often the more aggressive. I had to pull the bait away from those small fries and move it in front of the grandma sunny. But that was also when I found out why that big sunny was still around. It was frustrating to watch this grandma sunfish hang below the edge of the hole, casually eyeing my bait but not touching it. Then slowly she'd turn and swim away, all the while the little ones were fighting to be hooked.

Crossing Open Water

EVEN AFTER THE ICE MELTED FROM THE SHORE, there was often safe ice out on the main part of the lake, and one only needed a board or ladder to bridge the open water to get to that ice. As the gap widened, Ron and I would often use my flat-bottomed duck boat to scoot across the gap to the solid ice. We may have looked stupid, but we caught fish.

Ice Fishing on the Mississippi River

THE MISSISSIPPI IS HOME TO A GREAT NUMBER of fish and some really big ones. I was ice fishing for walleyes one day when I hooked into a northern and fought it on a light line. I had the head of the fish above water when the line broke, and the fish slid back into the hole. When its

212

nose was just below the water, it made a powerful surge and actually shot back out of the hole. I grabbed at it and caught it midway on the body. It was that far out of the water. It weighed two and three-quarters pounds. This was really cool because, not only had I caught the fish, but I had my lure back, too.

In Sartell, Minnesota, there's a dam across the Mississippi. It produces electricity on one side and has flumes on the other to bypass excess river flow. The water going through the power plant keeps that

area of the river open, and with no water coming over the flumes on the other side, it freezes over with enough ice to support fishing.

Ron and I were fishing there, with several others, when someone walked out on a railing above the dam, motioning and yelling for us to get off the river. We really couldn't hear what he was saying, but his frantic motions sure indicated that we should move quickly. I couldn't see what the rush was, and I was just having a walleye consider taking my bait. When I finally got my walleye, everyone was off the ice except for Ron, who was waiting for me. I headed to the shore, but that's when I noticed that the level of the ice had dropped eighteen inches, making it difficult to climb the bank.

The next day in the paper was a story of the hero of the power plant who had maybe saved some lives by getting ice fishermen off the ice. The power plant had some problems where the water discharge tunnels were closed. This caused the level of water to drop below the dam. There would have been no danger, though, as the ice would have just gone aground on the rocks and stopped there. I could have fished a little longer.

Not Going to Waste

NEVER WANTING THINGS TO GO TO WASTE, having eaten muskrat, raccoon, woodchuck, porcupine, among others, I wasn't about to let some perch lay on the ice.

Fishing on Mille Lacs with Chuck and his son, Joel, some fishermen had departed the lake, leaving some perch on the ice.

As I was picking them up, Joel was laughing, thinking it odd, and it has been an ongoing joke since, like, "The walleyes weren't biting, but I picked up a few perch."

Author's Note: These are just a few of the memories I have of fishing in Minnesota lakes and rivers. At some point, I hope to have a book devoted to my fishing experiences in Alaska. It will include the interesting and humorous stories from other Alaskans, fishing guides, and visiting fishermen and information about the tremendous beauty of Alaska as well.